THE POWER OF
SELF-LEADERSHIP

The Power of Self-Leadership

The Path to Unleash Your Talents, Strengths, and Superpowers

Douglas L. Schmidt

For information about permission to reproduce selections of this book email: DougSchmidt1955@GMail.com

ISBN (paperback): 979-8-9927080-0-4
ISBN (ebook): 979-8-9927080-1-1

Book design and production by www.AuthorSuccess.com

To my Mom and Dad

Contents

INTRODUCTION   1

CHAPTER 1:   Self-Leadership and Discovery   7

CHAPTER 2:   Discover Your Talents, Strengths, and Superpowers   31

CHAPTER 3:   Goal Setting Tips and Techniques   53

CHAPTER 4:   Developing Your Learning Superpower   68

CHAPTER 5:   Personal SWOT Analysis—Your Strategic Tool for Success   89

CHAPTER 6:   Developing A Growth and Grit Mindset   108

CHAPTER 7:   Developing Mental Strength   123

CHAPTER 8:   Overcoming Procrastination—Tools and Techniques   146

CHAPTER 9:   Developing SMART Habits   162

CHAPTER 10:   SMART Networking for Personal and Professional Success   179

CHAPTER 11:   Dealing With Toxic People   197

CHAPTER 12:   Putting It All Together: Self-Leadership, Self-Discovery, and Self-Empowerment   211

Sources   227

Acknowledgments   237

INTRODUCTION

To the Readers

Welcome to a transformative journey beyond this book's pages—a journey of self-leadership, self-discovery, and personal triumph. In the following chapters, you will embark together on a path that unveils the extraordinary potential within you, empowering you to overcome obstacles and embrace a life of purpose and resilience.

This book is a collection of lessons, tools, and techniques I gathered from mentors/role models, subject matter experts, books, and other resources during my journey. It is meant to inspire you to take control and manage your life and embrace the rewards that come with the journey of self-leadership and discovery.

Who Is This Book For

The Power of Self-Leadership is for anyone who wants to take control of their own life and become the best version of themselves. You will unleash your talents, strengths, and superpowers. Make empowered choices and create a life of purpose and fulfillment by leading yourself effectively.

- **Professionals:** Those looking to improve their career prospects by developing strong leadership skills, increasing self-motivation, and taking proactive steps toward their goals.
- **Aspiring Leaders:** Individuals aiming to step into leadership roles must understand how to lead themselves before they can effectively lead others.

+ **Entrepreneurs:** People running or starting their businesses who need to cultivate discipline, resilience, and a growth mindset to overcome challenges.
+ **Students and Young Adults:** Those at the beginning of their journey who want to build a foundation of self-discipline, confidence, and goal setting to achieve success.
+ **Personal Development Enthusiasts:** Individuals committed to self-improvement seeking strategies to enhance their decision-making, emotional intelligence, and overall well-being.
+ **Anyone Facing Life Transitions:** People experiencing significant changes, such as career shifts, personal loss, or major life decisions, need guidance on navigating these challenges with confidence and purpose.

How To Use This Book

This book serves as a reference guide for your roadmap of self-leadership and discovery. Each chapter gives concepts, resources, and ideas you can use to benefit.

I recommend choosing one or two ideas, habits, or concepts from each chapter in the lists provided. Trying to do all the concepts listed in the chapters can be overwhelming and result in inaction.

You do not have to do them all at the same time. Please keep it simple. One or two can change your life. You can go back to each chapter when you need ideas and motivation for the challenges and obstacles you face or feel stuck in being unable to solve.

Unleash Your Talents, Strengths, and Superpowers

"Unleash your talents, strengths, and superpowers" is a phrase that refers to the process of identifying, developing, and fully utilizing the unique abilities and qualities that make you exceptional.

You have a wealth of superpowers, strengths, and talents inside you waiting to be developed. This book is your compass for identifying, nurturing, and leveraging your innate abilities. You will learn how understanding and using your superpowers, talents, and strengths can propel you forward, creating a life that aligns with your aspirations.

- **Talents**: These are your natural abilities or aptitudes—things you are inherently good at. Unleashing your talents means recognizing what you naturally excel at and finding ways to use these skills in your personal and professional life.

- **Strengths**: Strengths are the areas where you have developed expertise or competence through practice, learning, and experience. Unleashing your strengths involves honing these areas further and applying them strategically to achieve your goals.

- **Superpowers**: Superpowers refer to your most exceptional abilities—those rare skills or qualities that set you apart. These might combine your talents and strengths, amplified by passion or a unique perspective. Unleashing your superpowers means fully embracing and leveraging these standout qualities to make a significant impact.

Together, the phrase encourages you to recognize your potential, nurture it, and use it to achieve your total capacity. It's about breaking through self-imposed limits, overcoming obstacles, and confidently bringing your best to every challenge or opportunity.

As you delve into the following chapters, consider this book a trusted companion on your personal development journey. Each page is designed to inspire, empower, and guide you toward a more self-aware, purposeful, and resilient version of yourself.

Embrace the adventure that awaits within these words, and let this book catalyze the transformative journey you have been waiting for.

Explore the Depths of Self-Leadership

Have you ever wondered about the untapped reservoirs of your potential? Prepare to embark on a journey of self-discovery that transcends boundaries and unlocks the unique strengths that make you extraordinary. Uncover the layers of your authentic self and learn how embracing your true nature can bring about a profound and personal transformation.

"*The Power of Self-Leadership*" refers to the ability and capacity to guide and manage oneself effectively. It involves taking responsibility for one's actions, decisions, and growth and is crucial to personal and professional development.

Key Elements of Self-Leadership

+ **Self-Awareness:** Understanding your strengths, weaknesses, values, and motivations. Recognizing your emotions and how they influence your behavior and decisions.

+ **Self-Motivation:** Setting personal goals and finding intrinsic motivation to achieve them. Maintaining focus and discipline to pursue your goals.

+ **Self-Regulation:** Managing your emotions, thoughts, and behaviors in different situations. Exercising self-control and making deliberate choices that align with your values and goals.

+ **Accountability:** Taking responsibility for your actions and their outcomes. Be honest with yourself about your progress and areas for improvement.

+ **Goal Setting and Planning:** Defining clear, achievable goals and developing strategies to reach them. Prioritizing tasks and managing time effectively.

+ **Resilience and Adaptability:** Overcoming setbacks and challenges with perseverance and flexibility. Learning from experiences and adapting to change.

+ **Continuous Learning and Growth:** Seeking personal and professional development opportunities, embracing feedback, and using it to improve and evolve.

Benefits of Self-Leadership

+ **Enhanced Self-Awareness**: Understanding your strengths, weaknesses, values, and motivations can help you make more informed decisions and set realistic goals.
+ **Improved Relationships**: Being aware of your emotions and triggers allows you to communicate more effectively and empathetically with others, fostering stronger interpersonal relationships.
+ **Increased Confidence**: Knowing yourself well can boost your self-esteem and confidence, as you are more likely to trust your instincts and abilities.
+ **Better Decision-Making**: Self-discovery helps clarify what is important to you, enabling you to make choices that align with your values and long-term goals.
+ **Personal Growth**: Encourages continuous learning and development, leading to a more fulfilling and purposeful life.
+ **Greater Resilience**: Understanding your coping mechanisms and stress triggers can help you develop strategies to manage adversity more effectively.
+ **Enhanced Creativity and Innovation**: You can use your unique perspective to develop creative solutions and ideas when you understand your thought processes and preferences.

Unlock Your Leadership Potential

Embracing *The Power of Self-Leadership* implies a comprehensive approach to personal development. It means actively shaping your life path by deeply understanding yourself and leading yourself with intention and purpose. This approach allows you to live authentically, achieve your goals, and navigate life's challenges confidently and clearly.

Discover the leader within you. This book is not just about leadership in the traditional sense; it is about self-leadership—the ability to guide your life with intention and purpose. You will learn practical strategies to navigate challenges, make empowered decisions, and lead yourself toward a more fulfilling existence.

**Unleash Your Talents, Strengths,
and Superpowers.
You've got this!
Enjoy the journey!**

CHAPTER 1

Self-Leadership and Discovery

"You have power over your mind, not outside events. Realize this, and you will find strength."

Marcus Aurelius—Roman Emperor and Stoic Philosopher

Welcome to the Journey

Welcome to your self-leadership and discovery journey, a less-traveled path but profoundly impactful. In the whirlwind of life, we often find ourselves pulled in myriad directions: meeting external expectations, chasing professional milestones, and navigating the demands of personal relationships. Amidst this external chaos, a powerful force exists within us—a force that, when harnessed, can shape our destinies and redefine our narratives. This is your power, your ability to steer your life in your desired direction.

Imagine embarking on a journey where every challenge tests your limits, and every setback pushes you to dig deeper within yourself. As the hero of this story, you start with uncertainty but a deep desire to make a difference. Along the way, you encounter obstacles that demand more than skill—they require courage, faith, and a strong sense of values. Courage is developed as you face your fears head-on, realizing that true bravery isn't the absence of fear but the determination to act despite it. Faith grows as you learn to trust in the process, believing that every step, no matter how difficult, leads you to where you need to be. Your values become your compass, guiding you through the most challenging decisions and helping you stay true to yourself. Through this journey, you emerge not just as a survivor but as a leader who has forged a path through adversity with integrity, strength, and an unshakeable belief in the power of perseverance.

In the following pages, you are invited to embark on a profoundly personal journey of self-leadership and discovery within your very being. This is not a traditional leadership manual prescribing external strategies or one-size-fits-all solutions. Instead, it is an odyssey of self-discovery, a pilgrimage into the depths of your values, strengths, and aspirations. Self-leadership and discovery are not about changing who you are; it is about becoming more authentic and wielding that authenticity as a powerful instrument for personal and professional success.

As we venture into this unique and transformative journey together, you will uncover the tools, insights, and wisdom to navigate the complexities of life with clarity, purpose, and resilience. Whether you are a seasoned professional, an aspiring leader, or seeking a meaningful shift in your narrative, self-leadership and discovery principles are universally applicable. So, let us embark on this transformative voyage, where the compass is your innermost self, and the destination is a life led by intention, impact, and fulfillment.

Daily challenges, whether in business or personal life, are everyday experiences. These challenges sometimes seem overwhelming and frustrating, and I understand how that feels. However, regardless of your journey, it is essential to remember that resources are always available to help you overcome these challenges and achieve your goals and intentions. This book looks to help you in your journey.

Self-leadership and discovery encompass the ability to take charge of your life, make conscious choices, and guide yourself toward achieving personal and professional goals. It involves the internal processes, skills, and behaviors you influence and direct yourself, fostering autonomy, motivation, and a sense of purpose. Self-leadership is about using your strengths, values, and aspirations to navigate challenges, make informed decisions, and continuously pursue growth and development.

Critical components of self-leadership and discovery include self-awareness, self-regulation, goal setting, emotional intelligence, and an initiative-taking mindset. This approach empowers you to shape your destinies, take responsibility for your actions, and create a meaningful and fulfilling life.

"One can have no smaller or greater mastery than mastery of oneself."

Leonardo Da Vinci—Italian Polymath

The Why—Key Benefits of Self-Leadership and Discovery

Self-leadership and discovery are grounded in compelling reasons, often called 'the why of self-leadership and discovery.' Understanding these motivations helps you recognize the importance and benefits of cultivating self-leadership and discovery skills. Self-leadership and discovery offer many benefits, empowering you to take control of your life, make informed decisions, and achieve personal and professional success.

The benefits include gaining insight into personal values, strengths, and passions, which can lead to more informed and fulfilling life choices. Self-discovery also fosters emotional intelligence and resilience, enhancing one's ability to navigate challenges and build authentic relationships. Self-leadership and discovery are essential for personal growth and realizing one's full potential.

Benefits of Self-Leadership and Discovery:

+   **Increased Self-Awareness:** Self-leadership involves deeply understanding your values, strengths, weaknesses, and motivations, leading to heightened self-awareness.

+   **Enhanced Decision-Making:** Practicing self-leadership equips you to make informed, effective decisions that align with your goals and values.

+   **Greater Motivation and Drive:** Self-leadership fosters intrinsic motivation by allowing you to connect actions to personal goals and values, fueling a sense of purpose.

+   **Improved Emotional Intelligence:** Self-leadership contributes to the development of emotional intelligence, allowing you to navigate your emotions and interpersonal relationships more effectively.

+   **Effective Goal Setting:** Self-leadership allows you to set meaningful and achievable goals, creating a personal and professional development roadmap.

+   **Resilience in the Face of Challenges:** Self-leadership equips you with the tools to navigate challenges, bounce back from setbacks, and keep a positive outlook.

+   **Increased Accountability:** Self-leadership encourages taking responsibility and accountability for your actions, fostering a proactive personal and professional growth approach.

+   **Enhanced Time Management:** Self-leadership practices can help you manage your time efficiently, prioritize tasks, and focus on activities that align with your goals.

+   **Improved Communication Skills:** Self-leadership involves effective communication with oneself and others, improving relationships, collaboration, and conflict resolution.

- **Adaptability and Flexibility:** Self-leadership encourages adaptability and flexibility in the face of change, allowing you to embrace new opportunities and navigate uncertainty.

- **Optimal Stress Management:** Practicing self-leadership develops effective stress management techniques, promoting overall well-being and mental health.

- **Empowerment and Independence:** Self-leadership empowers you to take initiative, make choices independently, and lead you toward your desired outcomes.

- **Continuous Learning and Growth:** A self-leadership mindset fosters a commitment to continuous learning, personal development, and the pursuit of new skills and knowledge.

- **Positive Impact on Others:** Effective leaders often inspire and positively influence those around them, contributing to a positive and productive environment.

- **Building a Fulfilling Life:** Self-leadership is instrumental in creating a fulfilling life by aligning your actions with personal values and aspirations.

Self-leadership and discovery are transformative and empowering practices that help you and have a ripple effect on your relationships, work, and the broader community. They enable you to lead from within, fostering a holistic and sustainable approach to personal and professional success.

"The hero's journey is not about becoming a superhero but discovering the hero within ourselves."

—Joseph Campbell—Author—
The Hero's Journey

Reframe Your Journey as A Hero's Journey

Reframing your self-leadership journey as a Hero's Journey can offer powerful benefits by providing a structured narrative that helps you understand and navigate life's challenges. Viewing yourself as the hero in your own story allows you to recognize the significance of each phase—whether it's the call to adventure, facing obstacles, or achieving transformation. This perspective encourages resilience by helping you see challenges as essential trials that lead to growth and self-discovery. It also fosters a sense of purpose as you understand that your struggles are part of a larger narrative leading to fulfillment and wisdom. By seeing your life through the lens of the Hero's Journey, you can cultivate a mindset of empowerment, where setbacks become learning opportunities, and every stage of your journey contributes to your ultimate success.

The Hero's Journey is a timeless narrative framework that traces the transformative path of a protagonist as they venture from their familiar world into the unknown, face formidable challenges, and emerge changed. In his book, *The Hero with a Thousand Faces*, Joseph Campbell describes how, "The hero is the one who has been able to battle past his own personal and regional limitations." It begins with the hero in their Ordinary World, unaware of the adventure awaiting them. The Call to Adventure disrupts your routine, compelling you to embark on a quest, though you may initially resist.

Using the hero's journey as a framework for your self-leadership provides a roadmap to begin the adventure of self-leadership and discovery.

Here's How Your Journey Might Look:

+ **The Ordinary World:** Personally or professionally, you start in your familiar environment. You are accustomed to your everyday work and life's routine, goals, and challenges.

+ **The Call to Adventure:** The call to adventure in a context could be a new opportunity, challenge, or goal, whether professional or personal, within your community, family organization, or industry. It may come as a promotion, a new project, a leadership role, or a chance to tackle a significant problem or opportunity. It could also be a change in your family, community, or personal life.

- **Refusal of the Call:** You might initially hesitate or feel uncertain about stepping out of your comfort zone to pursue this new opportunity. You may question whether you have the skills, experience, or resources necessary to succeed in this new endeavor.

- **Meeting the Mentor:** To navigate this unfamiliar territory, you seek guidance and support from mentors, colleagues, friends, or experts who have experience and insights to offer. These mentors provide advice, encouragement, and valuable perspective as you prepare for the journey.

- **Crossing the Threshold:** With the guidance of your mentors and a growing sense of confidence, you decide to embrace the new opportunity and step into unfamiliar territory. You leave behind the safety of your Ordinary World and embark on a journey of growth and discovery.

- **Tests, Allies, and Enemies:** Along the journey, you meet various challenges, obstacles, and opportunities for learning. You forge alliances with colleagues, friends, or mentors who support and collaborate while facing resistance, competition, or setbacks from others or in the environment you encounter.

- **Approach to the Inmost Cave:** As you progress, you approach significant milestones, goals, or obstacles that are the heart of your journey. These may include high-stakes projects, leadership opportunities, career transitions, or moments of decision-making that require courage and determination.

- **The Ordeal:** You confront your most significant challenges, make tough decisions, and push through moments of uncertainty or adversity. This could involve overcoming failures, navigating conflicts, or persevering through setbacks that test your resolve and resilience.

+ **Reward (Seizing the Sword):** After facing your ordeal, you emerge stronger, wiser, and more capable than before. You achieve significant milestones, gain valuable experience, and acquire new skills, knowledge, or insights that position you for success in your career or personal life.

+ **The Road Back:** With your achievements and newfound wisdom, you integrate your experiences and prepare to apply them to future endeavors. You may reflect on your journey, consolidate your learnings, and consider leveraging your strengths and experiences as you progress to achieve your goals or vision.

+ **Resurrection:** You undergo a personal transformation, emerging from your professional or personal challenges with a renewed sense of purpose, confidence, and direction. You embody the qualities of someone who has faced adversity and grown more potent.

+ **Return with the Elixir:** Armed with your experiences, insights, and achievements, you return to your environment as a more effective, influential, and empowered human being. You share your knowledge, mentor others, and contribute to the success of your organization, family, or community while pursuing new goals and challenges on your ongoing self-leadership journey.

With the guidance of mentors and allies, you navigate through the unknown, learning valuable lessons and gaining insights that shape your journey. As you overcome challenges and embrace your true potential, you emerge transformed, equipped with the knowledge and experience to lead others and make a meaningful impact in your family, community, organization, or industry. Through the hero's journey and self-leadership, you discover your inner strengths, unlock your full potential, and embark on a path of growth and success.

Discovering Self-Leadership and Discovery

By effectively leading yourself, you can navigate life's challenges with confidence and resilience and become the best version of yourself. Embarking on the self-leadership and discovery journey requires dedication, self-awareness, and a commitment to continuous improvement. These to-dos can serve as a roadmap as you discover and lead yourself toward personal and professional fulfillment.

Self-leadership and discovery are essential for personal growth and development, and the acronym **SELF** encompasses its fundamental principles.

- **Self-awareness** enables you to understand your strengths, weaknesses, values, and emotions.

- **Empowerment** encourages you to take ownership of your actions and decisions, fostering a sense of autonomy and responsibility.

- **Learning** reminds you of the importance of continuous growth and adaptation.

- **Focus** helps you prioritize your goals and achieve desired outcomes.

Steps on Your Journey

A self-leadership journey requires a thoughtful approach to personal growth and development. Establishing a clear set of actionable steps is essential to help build a strong foundation of self-awareness, discipline, and resilience to navigate this path effectively. These steps include a variety of practices aimed at improving your ability to lead yourself with clarity and confidence, such as setting meaningful goals, practicing self-reflection, embracing continuous learning, and managing your time effectively. By systematically addressing these key areas, you can achieve personal and professional objectives and lead a more fulfilling and empowered life.

Steps to Guide You on the Journey of Self-Leadership and Discovery:

+ **Self-Reflection:** Take time to introspect and understand your values, beliefs, strengths, and areas for growth. Reflect on past experiences that have shaped you.

+ **Define Your Purpose and Goals:** Defining short-term and long-term goals that align with your purpose in life is essential. This will assist you in maintaining focus and prioritizing things that are truly important to you.

+ **Build Self-Awareness:** To become self-aware, it is crucial to continuously assess and understand your emotions, reactions, and thought patterns. Mindfulness is a powerful tool that can help you stay present and attentive to your thoughts and actions. Therefore, cultivate mindfulness as an essential habit to stay in control of your life.

+ **Create a Vision Board:** A vision board is a powerful tool for visualizing and achieving your goals. Use images, quotes, and symbols that resonate with your aspirations. This visual reminder can motivate and inspire you to act.

+ **Develop a Positive Mindset:** Challenge negative self-talk, embrace self-compassion, and learn from setbacks to grow.

+ **Set Clear Boundaries:** Setting boundaries and prioritizing activities that align with your goals and values is essential.

+ **Master Time Management:** Prioritizing tasks, setting realistic deadlines, and organizing schedules effectively contribute to increased productivity and goal achievement.

+ **Embrace Failure as a Learning Opportunity:** Shift your perspective on failure and consider it a natural part of the learning process. Analyze setbacks, learn from them, and adjust your approach to see them as opportunities for growth.

+ **Practice Delegation:** Collaborating and delegating tasks to others they can handle is crucial. Doing this will allow you to concentrate on high-priority activities and goals.

+ **Hold Yourself Accountable:** Set up accountability mechanisms. This involves tracking progress, celebrating achievements, and taking responsibility for decisions and actions.

+ **Seek Continuous Learning:** Committing to lifelong learning is essential. This can be achieved by reading books, attending workshops, and engaging in activities that broaden one's knowledge and skills. Embracing a growth mindset is vital.

+ **Connect with Mentors and Peers:** Surround yourself with positive influences. Seek mentors who can guide you and connect with peers with similar goals. A supportive network is invaluable.

+ **Regularly Reassess Your Goals:** Periodically reassess and adjust your goals based on changing circumstances or personal growth. Adaptability is key to sustained self-leadership.

+ **Practice Gratitude:** Cultivate a mindset of gratitude. Regularly acknowledge and appreciate the positive aspects of your life. Gratitude can enhance your overall well-being.

+ **Live in Alignment with Your Values:** Ensure your actions align. Make decisions that resonate with your core beliefs, fostering authenticity and integrity in your self-leadership journey.

You can better navigate adversity and uncertainty by understanding yourself, including strengths, weaknesses, and passions. The journey of self-leadership and discovery builds inner strength, fosters independence, and encourages personal growth, enabling you to face difficulties with a sense of purpose and control.

"Jason Kelce exemplifies the grit and heart of a true leader—tough on the field and compassionate off it. His journey reminds us that success is not just about talent but also about resilience, teamwork, and the courage to lead by example."

Jason Kelce, Professional Football Player—Hero's Journey

Jason Kelce, the recently retired star center for the Philadelphia Eagles, embodies a compelling Hero's Journey that highlights his transformation from an underestimated player to a respected leader in the NFL, Super Bowl champion, and inspirational figure.

He is a role model for many people, including myself. The following is a comparison of Jason Kelce's journey with the concept of the Hero's Journey.

1. **The Ordinary World:** Jason Kelce grew up in Cleveland Heights, Ohio, in a sports-loving family. Despite being athletic, he was often overlooked due to his size and non-traditional build for a football player. Kelce's early football career at Cleveland Heights High School was solid but unremarkable, leaving him somewhat under the radar for college scouts.

2. **The Call to Adventure:** The call to adventure came when Kelce decided to walk on at the University of Cincinnati as a linebacker. His transition to playing center, a position he had never played, marked the beginning of his journey into uncharted territory. This required learning new skills and adapting to a completely different role on the field.

3. **Refusal of the Call:** Kelce faced doubts and challenges early in his college career. The center switch was difficult, and he was not immediately successful. There were moments when he questioned whether he could succeed in this new role, particularly given his smaller stature for an offensive lineman.

4. **Meeting the Mentor:** Throughout his journey, Kelce received mentorship from coaches who recognized his potential and helped him refine his skills. His college coaches guided his development, helping him become a reliable and versatile lineman. In the NFL, veteran players and coaches continued to mentor him, contributing to his growth as a player and a leader.

5. **Crossing the Threshold:** Kelce crossed the threshold when the Philadelphia Eagles drafted him in the sixth round of the 2011 NFL Draft. This was a pivotal moment, as he entered the highly competitive world of professional football, with many doubting whether a sixth-round pick with his size could succeed in the NFL.

6. **Tests, Allies, and Enemies:** Kelce's NFL career has been filled with tests, including proving his worth as a starting center, overcoming injuries, and dealing with the pressure of professional sports. His allies were his teammates, coaches, and family, particularly his brother Travis Kelce, who provided support and inspiration. His enemies were the critics who doubted his abilities and the physical toll of playing in the NFL.

7. **Approach to the Inmost Cave:** The approach to the inmost cave occurred as Kelce became a key leader on the Eagles, particularly during the 2017 season. The Eagles' journey to Super Bowl LII was fraught with challenges, including losing their starting quarterback, Carson Wentz. As one of the team's leaders, Kelce had to step up, rally the team, and maintain focus amidst adversity.

8. **The Ordeal:** The ordeal culminated in Super Bowl LII, where the Eagles faced the New England Patriots, led by Tom Brady. Kelce and the Eagles had to overcome the pressure of playing against one of the most successful franchises in NFL history. Kelce's performance as the center, anchoring the offensive line, was critical in the Eagles' victory.

9. **The Reward:** The reward was winning Super Bowl LII, the first in the Philadelphia Eagles' history. Kelce's emotional and iconic victory speech at the parade, where he famously dressed as a Mummer (Mummers

are a grand Philadelphia tradition of young men reveling during the Christmas-New Years period) and passionately defended his team and city, solidified his place as a Philadelphia legend. This victory and his leadership earned him respect and admiration across the NFL.

10. **The Road Back:** Kelce continued his NFL career with renewed purpose and leadership after the Super Bowl. He faced the challenge of maintaining high performance and leadership, even as the Eagles navigated the ups and downs of subsequent seasons. He also took on the responsibility of mentoring younger players.

11. **The Resurrection:** Kelce's resurrection is ongoing as he plays at an elite level, defying the odds and remaining one of the best centers in the NFL. His resilience, leadership, and commitment to his team have kept him at the top of his game, earning multiple Pro Bowl selections and solidifying his legacy.

12. **Return with the Elixir:** The elixir Kelce brings back is his example of perseverance, leadership, and passion for the game. He is a symbol of what it means to overcome obstacles, to lead with heart, and to give everything to his team and community. His journey inspires his teammates, countless fans, and aspiring athletes who look up to him as a role model.

Jason Kelce's Hero's Journey is a story of grit, determination, and heart. From an overlooked college player to an NFL champion and leader, his path exemplifies the power of belief, hard work, and leadership in achieving greatness. As of the writing of this book, Jason Kelce retired in March 2024.

The greatest obstacles to self-leadership are self-doubt and fear of the unknown. Overcoming them requires courage, reflection, and a commitment to growth.

Obstacles To Self-Leadership and Discovery

Self-leadership and discovery, the ability to guide ourselves in achieving personal and professional goals, we can face various obstacles. Overcoming these challenges is essential for personal growth and success. To overcome obstacles and succeed, we must have self-reflection and unwavering resilience, set clear goals, and cultivate a positive mindset through effective self-leadership.

Face them with a heart full of resilience, a mind brimming with optimism, and the unwavering belief that you can achieve greatness. You have within you an indomitable spirit that can triumph over any challenge. Keep pushing forward and remember that your brightest moments often arise from the darkest hours. The stars shine most brilliantly against the backdrop of the night sky. Your light will shine through the darkness, guiding you to the victory that awaits on the other side of every obstacle.

Common Obstacles to Self-Leadership and Discovery:

+ **Lack of Self-Awareness:** Effective self-leadership requires self-awareness to set meaningful goals and align decisions with personal values.

+ **Fear of Failure:** Fear of failure can prevent you from taking risks or pursuing goals. Embracing failure as part of the learning process is essential for self-leadership.

+ **Procrastination:** Procrastination can hinder progress and prevent achieving goals, making it a significant obstacle to self-leadership.

+ **Lack of Goal Clarity:** Unclear or vague goals make creating a roadmap for self-leadership challenging. Clearly defined and achievable goals provide direction and motivation.

- **Ineffective Time Management:** Poor time management can hinder productivity and progress. Developing time management skills is vital for effective self-leadership.

- **Negative Self-Talk:** Negative self-talk and self-limiting beliefs can undermine confidence and hinder personal development. Cultivating a positive mindset is essential for effective self-leadership.

- **Resistance to Change:** Avoiding change can hinder personal development, but embracing and adapting to new circumstances is vital to effective self-leadership.

- **Lack of Resilience:** Resilience is the ability to recover from difficulties. Without resilience, you may struggle to navigate challenges and persist through adversity.

- **Difficulty Saying No:** Over-committing tasks or obligations can lead to burnout and hinder progress toward personal goals. A key aspect of self-leadership is learning to set boundaries and say no when necessary.

- **Perfectionism:** Prioritizing progress over perfection is essential to avoid unrealistic expectations and frustration, especially when practicing self-leadership.

- **Inability to Delegate:** Often, taking on too much responsibility without delegating tasks can overwhelm and hinder efficiency. Learning to delegate effectively is crucial for self-leadership.

- **Lack of Accountability:** Self-leadership requires holding oneself accountable for actions and outcomes. Taking responsibility, learning from mistakes, and making necessary adjustments becomes easier.

In life's journey, obstacles are not roadblocks but opportunities for your growth and resilience. Remember that every challenge you face is a chance to discover the strength that lives within you. Embrace adversity as a stepping stone toward your dreams, for it is through overcoming obstacles that you forge the path to success. Like a phoenix rising from the ashes, you have the power to appear stronger, wiser, and more resilient than ever before. Believe in your abilities, trust the process, and know that every setback is a setup for a remarkable comeback. Your journey is uniquely yours, and overcoming and learning from obstacles is a testament to your courage and determination.

Overcome and Use Obstacles to Your Advantage

Transform obstacles into stepping stones; use challenges as opportunities for growth. Every setback is a setup for a greater comeback, and within adversity lies the potential to forge a stronger, more resilient version of yourself. Equip yourself with powerful strategies to overcome obstacles and transform them into stepping stones to success.

Strategies To Overcome Obstacles:

+ **Embrace a Growth and Grit Mindset:** View your obstacles as personal and professional development opportunities. Believe your challenges are chances to learn, adapt, and become stronger. This mindset shift will lay the foundation for using your obstacles as learning experiences.

+ **Reframe Challenges as Opportunities:** Instead of seeing obstacles as roadblocks, reframe them as chances to highlight your problem-solving skills, resilience, and determination. Your ability to find solutions is a testament to your capabilities. Ask yourself, "How can I use this situation to my advantage?"

+ **Seek Learning in Adversity:** Every obstacle carries a lesson. Approach challenges with a curious mindset, looking to understand what you can learn from the experience. The knowledge gained can be invaluable even if the outcome could be better.

+ **Set Specific Goals:** Define clear goals for overcoming obstacles. Having a target to work towards can provide motivation and a sense of direction, helping you focus your efforts constructively.

+ **Break Down the Challenge:** Large obstacles can feel overwhelming. Break them into smaller, manageable tasks. Tackling each component can make the challenge seem less daunting and more achievable.

+ **Foster Adaptability:** Obstacles often require adapting to new situations. Cultivate flexibility and willingness to adjust your strategies based on changing circumstances. Remember, your resilience is your greatest strength in the face of change.

+ **Tap into Creativity:** Challenges stimulate creative thinking. Explore innovative solutions and consider unconventional approaches to overcome obstacles. Sometimes, the most unique solutions yield the best results.

+ **Build Resilience:** Obstacles test your resilience and ability to bounce back. Embrace challenges as opportunities to strengthen your emotional resilience, which can serve you well in various aspects of life.

+ **Leverage Support Networks:** Seek advice and support from mentors, peers, or professionals who have faced similar obstacles. Their insights can provide fresh perspectives and practical strategies.

+ **Track Progress and Celebrate Wins:** Track your progress as you overcome obstacles. Celebrate small wins and milestones along the way. Recognizing your achievements can boost your motivation and confidence.

+ **Cultivate Patience:** Not all obstacles are overcome overnight. Cultivate patience and understand that the process might take time. Persistence and consistency will eventually lead to progress.

+ **Maintain a Positive Mindset:** Stay positive throughout the process. A positive attitude can improve your problem-solving abilities and help you keep perspective.

✦ **Focus on Self-Care:** Dealing with obstacles can be emotionally and mentally draining. Prioritize self-care to support your overall well-being and ensure you have the best mindset to tackle challenges.

Remember that overcoming obstacles adds to your repertoire of experiences, skills, and resilience. You transform setbacks into personal and professional growth opportunities by using barriers. Transform obstacles into stepping stones; use challenges as opportunities for growth. Every setback is a setup for a more significant comeback, and within adversity lies the potential to forge a stronger, more resilient version of yourself.

My Story—Writing this Book

Writing this book has been a transformative discovery, discipline, and growth journey. What began as a simple idea evolved into a deep exploration of self-leadership, fueled by countless hours of research, reflection, and persistence. Along the way, I confronted my challenges—procrastination, doubt, and the complexity of bringing my vision to life—but I pushed forward through consistent effort and commitment. The process taught me the power of words and the importance of resilience, focus, and personal accountability. In the end, crafting this book became as much about my development as it is about sharing a message of empowerment with others.

1. **The Ordinary World:** I began my career with a passion for sales and marketing. Still, like many, I faced the typical challenges of finding my voice, establishing my niche, and figuring out how to make a real difference. Despite my talents and experience, having both successes and failures, I felt somewhat confined by the limits of my choices and the opportunities later in my life. I felt stuck and frustrated.

2. **The Call to Adventure:** My call to adventure came when I decided to write a book in September 2023. I realized I had a story to tell based on my insights and experiences. I wanted to get the concepts, ideas, and insights out of my head and on paper. I intended that I could inspire and lead others.

3. **Refusal of the Call:** Initially, I hesitated. Writing a book, putting myself out there in a new way, or taking on this writing project seemed daunting. I questioned whether I had the time, energy, or right to pursue such ambitious goals. Procrastination, self-doubt, and the demands of daily life pulled me back. I had to keep paying my bills and set time aside to write this book. I was overwhelmed and doubted my abilities.

4. **Meeting the Mentor:** Fortunately, mentors and role models began to appear. My mentors and role models appeared in various forms—friends, books, influential figures, authors, and military veterans. These mentors helped me to see that my perspectives were valuable, that my experiences could inspire others, and that I had the tools to overcome the obstacles in my way. These role models and mentors helped me to overcome my self-doubt.

5. **Crossing the Threshold:** I crossed the threshold when fully committed to writing. I set aside time each day to commit to writing this book. I began waking up early to ride my bike at 5:00 a.m., using that time to clear my mind, generate new ideas, and plan my writing for the day. I studied how to write and developed a mind map and framework for each chapter.

6. **Tests, Allies, and Enemies:** As I embarked on this path, I faced numerous tests. Balancing writing with other responsibilities, paying bills, overcoming procrastination, and staying disciplined were constant challenges. I found allies—mentors, supportive colleagues, and a supportive audience. My enemies were internal doubts, distractions, and the uncertainty of whether I could write a book. Yet, each test made me stronger and more focused. If I became frustrated, I would take a break for a day or two. I hired a writing and publishing coach to assist my efforts.

7. **Approach to the Inmost Cave:** The inmost cave was represented by the most challenging part of my journey—a critical phase in my

book-writing process when I met an impasse and acknowledged I needed help. I hired a publishing and writing coach and mentor, Steve Harrison's Team, to assist and guide my efforts. I had to dig deep, rely on everything I had learned, and confront the fear of failure or rejection head-on

8. **The Ordeal:** The ordeal was pivotal when I faced a significant setback. I found that the original platform I was writing on was not the best one for me. I had to switch my writing platform to meet my needs better and transfer all my work to a different platform. It was a period of self-doubt and frustration. I wondered if I would ever get this book written. I had to decide on content, graphics, and the book cover. I had no experience in doing this. Fortunately, overcoming this ordeal required tapping into my inner resilience and creativity, pushing me through when it seemed easier to give up. My writing coaches and mentors encouraged me and supported me throughout this process. I was not stuck. I was moving forward.

9. **The Reward:** My reward came in tangible successes—my book looked like it would be finished. I had persevered and was patient, resulting in the gratification I could believe and see I could publish a book. This reward validated my efforts and proved that I was capable of much more than I had initially thought. The patience and perseverance were paying off.

10. **The Road Back:** I continued evolving, realizing the journey was ongoing. I started sharing my story more broadly, helping others on similar paths or taking on new challenges aligned with their growth. I received positive feedback from respected individuals in my network. The road back involved consolidating and using my gains as a foundation for future endeavors. I began looking for ways to share my concepts and ideas.

11. **The Resurrection:** The resurrection is seen in my transformation—I became more confident, capable, and influential. I was no longer just

a writer or content creator; I became a leader, an inspiration, and a voice others look up to. This transformation is evident in approaching new challenges with renewed purpose and resilience. I no longer felt stuck and frustrated.

12. **Return with the Elixir:** The elixir I bring back is my wisdom, experience, and the content I created. My book, my insights on self-leadership, overcoming procrastination, and my successes in business are all part of this elixir. I can share this with others, helping them navigate their journeys, inspiring them to push past their limits, and showing they can achieve greatness with determination and the right mindset.

My Hero's Journey is a testament to the power of perseverance, self-belief, and the courage to pursue your passions, even when the path is uncertain. It's a journey that transforms you and empowers others to embark on their heroic journeys.

> The Hero's Journey is a timeless blueprint for transformation, illustrating how ordinary individuals embark on extraordinary quests, face challenges, and return stronger with insights to share. It's a universal story of growth, resilience, and the power of self-discovery.

Summary

Self-leadership and discovery begin with mastering the self; it is the journey of navigating one's inner landscape with courage, integrity, and wisdom, inspiring others to embark on their voyage of self-discovery and growth.

You can reframe your journey as a heroic journey where you are the hero of the journey. You are empowered to navigate your path, overcome challenges, and achieve personal transformation.

Self-discovery is not a destination but a journey. You cannot achieve it in a day, a week, or a year. You can pursue it as you grow, change, and evolve. Self-discovery is not a linear path but a winding road. It is something other than something you can follow with a map, a guide, or a plan. You can explore it with curiosity, courage, and creativity.

Self-discovery is not a fixed state but a dynamic process. You cannot define it with a label, a role, or a category. It is something that you can express with your voice, your actions, and your passions. Self-discovery is not a final goal but a continuous opportunity. It is something other than what you can achieve with a certificate, a diploma, or a degree. It is something that you can enjoy with your mind, your heart, and your soul.

It is important to note that self-leadership and discovery is a highly individualized and ongoing process. Research on this topic reflects the complexity and diversity of human experiences. Different studies and approaches contribute to our understanding of self-leadership and discovery from various angles, and the field continues to evolve as new research emerges, validating your unique journey.

Embark on a transformative journey of self-leadership and discovery empowerment as we unravel the profound potential within you. This book explores the untapped reservoirs of leadership that lie dormant within you. Through this journey of self-awareness, resilience, and purpose, you will find the tools and inspiration to awaken your inner leader, instilling confidence and control in your life.

Amidst life's twists and turns, you find yourself standing at a crossroads, grappling with uncertainty and searching for direction. Feeling adrift in your career and personal life, you embark on a journey of self-leadership and discovery, determined to unlock your inner potential and take control of your destiny. Through introspection and reflection, you begin to unearth the qualities that define your essence and the values that guide your path. With newfound clarity, you embrace self-leadership principles, learn to trust your intuition, make empowered choices, and chart your course. As you cultivate self-awareness and confidence, you find yourself stepping into leadership roles at work, in your family, and in your community, inspiring others to do the same. With each challenge you face and triumph you celebrate, your self-leadership journey becomes a beacon of hope and empowerment, illuminating the path to personal fulfillment and success.

Action Steps

A good action step for the self-leadership and discovery journey is to practice self-reflection and journaling regularly.

Action Steps to Do It Effectively:

- **Set Aside Time Daily**: Dedicate at least fifteen minutes daily for self-reflection. Choose a quiet time, in the morning or before bed, when you can focus without interruptions.

- **Use Prompts**: Start with specific prompts to guide your journaling. Questions like "What did I learn about myself today?", "What challenges did I face and how did I manage them?" and "What am I grateful for?" can provide structure.

- **Identify Patterns and Insights**: Over time, review your journal entries to identify recurring themes, patterns in your behavior, and insights about your strengths and areas for improvement.

- **Set Goals and Action Plans**: Based on your reflections, set specific, measurable goals for your personal and professional development. Outline actionable steps to achieve these goals and track your progress regularly.

- **Seek Feedback**: Complement your self-reflection with feedback from trusted friends, mentors, or colleagues. This external perspective can offer valuable insights that you might overlook.

Your journey of unleashing and embracing your talents, strengths, and superpowers begins one action at a time. Be patient with yourself and your journey. Regular self-reflection and journaling help you stay attuned to your thoughts, emotions, and behaviors, fostering greater self-awareness and guiding you toward continuous personal growth and effective self-leadership.

CHAPTER 2

Discover Your Talents, Strengths, and Superpowers

"The two most important days in your life are the day you are born, and the day you find out why."

Mark Twain—Author

Understanding Your Talents, Strengths, and Superpowers

The concept of a 'personal superpower' is a metaphor for your unique strength or ability. This strength often relates to your talents, skills, or distinctive qualities. Unlike the supernatural abilities associated with comic book superheroes, a personal superpower is a positive and exceptional attribute that sets you apart.

It could be a combination of traits, such as creativity, empathy, resilience, leadership, or any other quality that contributes significantly to your success, well-being, or positive impact on others. Identifying and leveraging your superpowers can enhance self-awareness and guide personal and professional development.

Understanding and using your superpowers in a personal or professional context refers to recognizing and using your unique strengths, skills, and capabilities that set you apart. Just like superheroes have distinct abilities that make them extraordinary, you have innate qualities or developed skills that make you exceptional in certain areas.

Identifying and understanding your superpower involves self-awareness and a deep understanding of what makes you stand out. It could be a combination of skills, talents, or traits that you excel at and can use to contribute positively to your work, relationships, or personal goals. Once you understand your superpower, you can harness it to enhance your performance, make a meaningful impact, and align your actions with your strengths, leading to personal and professional success.

Discovering your superpowers is an ongoing process. It requires self-exploration, continuous learning, and accepting what makes you unique. Be patient and celebrate your journey. Write down where, when, and how you can use your superpowers. You will be surprised where your insights and wisdom will lead you.

As you explore your superpower, strengths, and talents, a remarkable transformation occurs—a heightened self-awareness propels you toward authenticity. These superpowers, talents, and strengths become guiding lights, empowering you to navigate challenges with resilience and grace.

While superpowers may encompass innate talents and extraordinary abilities, strengths and talents typically focus on developed skills and positive attributes that you can use to achieve your goals and fulfill their potential. Superpowers, strengths, and talents play a crucial role in personal and professional success, as they empower you to overcome challenges, make meaningful contributions, and lead fulfilling lives.

Superpowers, talents, and strengths are innate or developed abilities and qualities. They enable you to excel in various areas of life.

Breakdown of Each:

1. **Talents** are natural aptitudes or exceptional abilities in specific areas that you have. They can manifest in various forms, including intellectual, artistic, athletic, social, or practical skills. Talents often appear innate and can be recognized early in life, although they can be developed and refined through practice and experience.

- **Innate Abilities**: Talents are often seen as inherent strengths or natural gifts you are born with, differentiating them from skills typically acquired through training and practice.

- **Variety of Forms**: Talents can span a wide range of domains.

- **Artistic Talents**: Creativity in visual arts, music, dance, and writing.

- **Intellectual Talents**: Exceptional cognitive abilities in mathematics, science, and language.

- **Athletic Talents**: Physical prowess, coordination, and stamina in sports and physical activities.

- **Social Talents**: People skills such as empathy, communication, and leadership.

- **Practical Talents**: Technical skills, problem-solving abilities, and craftsmanship.

- **Practical Talents**: Technical skills, problem-solving abilities, and craftsmanship.

2. **Strengths** refer to the positive qualities, attributes, or capabilities that contribute to your overall well-being, success, and effectiveness in various aspects of life. These strengths are inherent to you and significantly shape your personality, behavior, and interactions with others.

   - **Skills and Competencies**: Your strengths are specific skills, competencies, or areas of expertise in which you excel. These strengths, developed through dedicated practice and experience, significantly shape your overall well-being, success, and effectiveness in various aspects of life.

   - **Positive Traits**: Strengths often align with positive character traits and virtues such as honesty, integrity, determination, and optimism.

- **Personal Attributes:** Strengths can also include attributes that contribute to success in various contexts, such as communication skills, organizational abilities, problem-solving skills, or emotional intelligence.

3. **Superpowers**, your unique, exceptional strengths or abilities, often reflect your distinct personality, character, or skill set. These superpowers, unique to you, can manifest in various aspects of life, contributing to personal success, fulfillment, and positive impact on others.

- **Innate Abilities:** Superpowers are often associated with innate talents or traits you are born with. These abilities might include exceptional intelligence, creativity, empathy, intuition, or physical prowess.

- **Unique Skills:** Superpowers can also encompass unique skills or talents that set you apart. For example, someone might have a remarkable talent for music, sports, mathematics, or problem-solving.

- **Extraordinary Qualities:** Superpowers may extend beyond conventional abilities and manifest in extraordinary qualities such as resilience, courage, adaptability, or the ability to inspire and lead others.

While superpowers may encompass innate talents and extraordinary abilities, strengths typically focus on developed skills and positive attributes that you can use to achieve your goals and fulfill their potential. Superpowers, strengths, and talents play a crucial role in personal and professional success, as they empower you to overcome challenges, make meaningful contributions, and lead fulfilling lives.

"We cannot solve our problems with the same thinking we used when we created them."

Albert Einstein

Benefits of Your Superpowers, Talents, and Strengths

To start this journey, we must not be super talented or famous. The most important concept is the start of the journey. Discovering your talents, strengths, and superpowers is not just about unlocking hidden talents but about unleashing your true potential and tapping into limitless possibilities.

Beyond personal triumphs, the ripple effect of recognizing and harnessing your superpowers, talents, and strengths extends to others, creating positive connections and fostering a community where your unique brilliance is celebrated. In the tapestry of life, understanding your superpowers weaves a narrative of empowerment, purpose, and the boundless possibilities that arise when you embrace the extraordinary within yourself.

Benefits Include:

+ **Boosted Confidence:** Recognizing and acknowledging your strengths is a powerful tool that enhances your confidence. This self-awareness empowers you to face challenges with self-assurance, fostering a positive self-image.

+ **Improved Focus:** Identifying your superpowers, talents, and strengths helps you focus on your strengths rather than fixating on your weaknesses. This focus allows you to channel your energy into areas where you can make the most significant impact.

+ **Effective Goal Setting:** Understanding your superpowers, talents, and strengths enables you to set goals that align with your strengths. This strategic approach increases the likelihood of achieving your goals and experiencing a sense of accomplishment.

+ **Better Decision-Making:** Knowing your superpowers, talents, and strengths clarifies decision-making. You can align your choices with your strengths, making decisions that play to your advantages and contribute to your success.

+ **Increased Job Satisfaction:** Using your superpowers, talents, and strengths at work can lead to greater job satisfaction in a professional context. You will feel more fulfilled and motivated when you engage in tasks that align with your superpowers, talents, and strengths.

+ **Effective Collaboration:** Understanding the superpowers, talents, and strengths of others in a team setting promotes effective collaboration. Team members can use each other's strengths, leading to a more cohesive and high-performing group.

+ **Personal Growth:** Identifying your superpowers, talents, and strengths is a journey of personal growth. As you become more aware of your superpowers, talents, and strengths, you may find opportunities for development and expansion, leading to continuous improvement.

+ **Improved Leadership:** For those in leadership roles, recognizing your superpowers, talents, and strengths allows you to lead authentically and use your strengths to inspire and guide others effectively.

+ **Adaptability and Resilience:** Knowing your superpowers, talents, and strengths helps you navigate challenges with resilience. Drawing on your strengths allows you to adapt to changing circumstances and find innovative solutions.

+ **Enhanced Communication:** Understanding your superpowers, talents, and strengths enables you to communicate your strengths more effectively. This can be valuable in job interviews, networking, and interpersonal relationships.

+ **Positive Impact on Well-Being:** Aligning your actions with your superpowers, talents, and strengths contributes to a sense of purpose and fulfillment, positively affecting your overall well-being and life satisfaction.

Identifying and leveraging your talents, strengths, and superpowers is a journey of self-discovery that can lead to a more fulfilling and successful life. It empowers you to maximize your potential and make meaningful contributions to your personal and professional spheres.

Harnessing your superpowers, talents, and strengths is about recognizing and using your unique strengths and abilities to achieve your goals and positively impact the world. It involves embracing your talents, passions, and values and using them to drive personal and professional growth. You can unlock your full potential, overcome obstacles, and navigate challenges confidently and resiliently. Whether creativity, leadership, empathy, or problem-solving skills, everyone has superpowers waiting to be discovered and unleashed. By embracing and harnessing these strengths and talents, you can cultivate a sense of purpose, fulfillment, and empowerment and create meaningful change for yourself and those around you.

Discover and Embrace Your Talents, Strengths, and Superpowers

Discovering your superpowers, talents, and strengths is just the beginning of an epic journey. Embrace the road ahead with courage, curiosity, and a relentless determination to unleash your full potential. Discovering your unique talents and strengths is the key to unlocking your 'superpowers.' This requires self-reflection and exploration, leading to a profound understanding of your capabilities.

Steps To Help You Identify and Unleash Your Talents, Strengths, and Superpowers:

+ **Self-Reflection:** Reflect on moments you felt in flow or accomplished and consider experiences and activities that bring you joy.

+ **Strengths Assessment:** Use strengths assessment tools such as the Clifton Strengths, Myers-Briggs, Strength Finders, VIA Survey of Character Strengths, or other personality assessments. These tools can provide insights into your strengths.

+ **Ask for Feedback:** It is essential to ask for feedback from those around you, such as friends, family, and colleagues. They may offer valuable insights into your strengths and talents that you might not be fully aware of.

+ **Passions and Interests:** Identify your interests and passions. Your natural talents often align with these activities. Lose track of time doing what you love.

- **Skills and Abilities:** Assess your skills and abilities. Identify areas where you excel and consider how these skills can be applied in various aspects of your life.

- **Challenge Yourself:** Take on new challenges or projects. Sometimes, your superpowers emerge when faced with unfamiliar situations that require you to tap into your innate strengths.

- **Seek Guidance:** Consider seeking guidance from mentors, coaches, or career advisors. They can help identify your strengths and hidden talents.

- **Journaling:** Keeping a journal to record your thoughts, feelings, and observations can help you identify patterns and recurring themes that highlight your strengths.

- **Values Alignment:** It is essential to consider your core values when identifying your strengths. Engaging in activities that align with your values can help you tap into those strengths.

- **Mindfulness Practices:** Engage in mindfulness practices like meditation or deep reflection to increase self-awareness.

- **Experiment and Explore:** Being open to new experiences and trying different activities, roles, or projects is essential. Exploring new things can help you uncover hidden talents and skills.

How to Identify Your Talents

These are your natural abilities or aptitudes—things you are inherently good at. Unleashing your talents means recognizing what you naturally excel at and finding ways to use these skills in your personal and professional life. Identifying your talents and abilities is a self-discovery process involving reflection, exploration, and feedback.

Steps to Uncover Your Talents and Natural Abilities:

+ **Reflect on Past Successes:** Think about moments when you excelled or felt particularly confident. What activities came easily to you? What were you doing when you received compliments or recognition? These moments often reveal your natural talents.

+ **Consider What Energizes You:** Pay attention to tasks or activities that energize and engage you. Talents are often connected to things you enjoy because they align with your innate abilities.

+ **Ask for Feedback:** Sometimes, others can see our talents more clearly than we can. Ask friends, family, colleagues, or mentors what they think you're naturally good at. Their perspectives can provide valuable insights.

+ **Analyze Patterns:** Look for patterns in your interests, hobbies, and tasks you tend to gravitate toward. For example, if you've always loved solving puzzles or organizing events, those might point to problem-solving or project management talents.

+ **Take Talent Assessments:** Various assessments are designed to help you identify your talents, such as the CliftonStrengths (formerly StrengthsFinder) assessment. These tools can provide structured insights into your natural abilities.

+ **Experiment and Explore:** Sometimes, you discover talents by trying new things. Step outside your comfort zone and explore different activities or roles. You might uncover a hidden talent by taking on a new challenge.

+ **Listen to Your Intuition:** Pay attention to your gut feelings. Sometimes, your intuition can guide you toward recognizing your talents, especially if you've always had a 'sense' that you're good at something.

+ **Reflect on What Comes Easily:** Talents often manifest as effortless skills. If you find yourself naturally excelling at something with little effort compared to others, it's likely a talent.

+ **Examine Childhood Interests:** Remember what you loved doing as a child. Childhood interests can provide clues about your innate talents, as they were likely pursued without external pressure or expectations.

+ **Notice Where You Add Value:** Consider where you consistently add value to your work or personal life. If people frequently turn to you for certain tasks or advice, it could signify a talent.

+ **Keep a Talent Journal:** Document your experiences, successes, and feedback. Over time, patterns will emerge that can help you pinpoint your talents.

Conclusion: Identifying your talents is an ongoing journey that requires self-awareness, exploration, and openness to feedback. Once identified, these talents can be nurtured and developed into strengths that significantly enhance your personal and professional life.

Identify Your Strengths

Identifying your personal and professional strengths is crucial for self-awareness and growth. Your strengths can be used whether in the family, communities, or organizations you work for. Everyone has leadership capabilities.

The strengths-based approach or perspective is a powerful philosophy that focuses on identifying and utilizing your positive qualities, assets, and strengths. This way of thinking and working aims to achieve personal growth, resilience, and success by building upon existing strengths and resources. It is a highly effective approach that has proven successful in helping individuals and groups achieve their goals and reach their full potential. So, if you want to improve your life or the lives of those around you, the strengths-based approach is worth considering.

The strengths-based philosophy is applied in various fields, including education, psychology, social work, counseling, and community development. For example, teachers and educators in education may identify students' strengths and tailor their teaching methods to support individual learning styles. Practitioners may explore clients' strengths in therapy or counseling to promote healing and resilience.

This approach contrasts with deficit-based approaches, which emphasize identifying and addressing problems, weaknesses, or shortcomings. The strengths-based philosophy aims to create a more positive and empowering framework for personal and collective growth by shifting the focus to strengths and building on existing resources.

Methods to Identify Your Strengths:

+ **Self-Reflection:** Reflect on situations where you succeeded or felt confident. Consider past achievements and think about what energizes you.

+ **Seek Feedback from Others:** Ask trusted individuals for input and use formal feedback mechanisms in professional settings.

+ **Take Strengths Assessments:** Use tools like Gallup CliftonStrengths and the Myers-Briggs Type Indicator to identify your natural strengths.

+ **Analyze Patterns in Your Performance:** Look for recurring themes in your accomplishments and identify skills in which you excel.

+ **Consider What Energizes You:** Pay attention to tasks that energize you, as they often indicate your strengths.

+ **Identify Areas of Fast Learning:** Take note of areas where you learn quickly and adapt to challenges.

+ **Look At What Others Rely On You For:** Pay attention to the tasks others seek help with, which can indicate areas of strength.

+ **Experiment and Try New Things:** To discover hidden strengths, test yourself in new situations.

+ **Evaluate Your Emotional Responses:** Pay attention to activities where you feel more confident, relaxed, and fulfilled.

+ **Keep a Strengths Journal:** Document your achievements, positive feedback, and empowering moments to reveal your personal and professional capabilities.

Final Thoughts: Identifying your strengths is a continuous process of self-discovery. By combining reflection, feedback, and structured assessments, you can clearly understand what you excel at and how to leverage those strengths for personal and professional growth.

Superpowers Identified

In a metaphorical sense, 'superpowers' refer to exceptional abilities or qualities you have that set you apart and enable you to excel in various aspects of life.

Developing your learning superpower starts with curiosity and a willingness to adapt. You unlock the limitless potential to grow and achieve when you embrace challenges, seek new knowledge, and refine your learning abilities.

Superpower Abilities and Qualities:

+ **Creativity:** The ability to generate original ideas, think outside the box, and solve problems innovatively.

+ **Resilience:** The ability to bounce back from setbacks, adversity, and challenges with strength and determination.

+ **Empathy:** The skill of understanding and sharing the feelings of others, fostering meaningful connections and relationships.

+ **Leadership:** The capability to inspire, motivate, and guide others toward common goals, driving positive change and growth.

+ **Adaptability:** The flexibility to adjust to new situations, environments, and changes quickly and gracefully.

+ **Communication:** Effectively expressing ideas, thoughts, and emotions fosters clarity, understanding, and collaboration.

+ **Grit:** The perseverance and passion to pursue long-term goals and aspirations despite obstacles and setbacks.

+ **Self-awareness:** The introspective ability to recognize one's superpowers, strengths, weaknesses, values, and emotions, leading to personal growth and development.

When cultivated and harnessed effectively, these superpowers can empower you to achieve extraordinary results and make a positive impact on your life and the lives of others.

"Your strengths are more than just actions—the qualities that make you feel empowered. Discovering them isn't solely about boosting performance; it's about recognizing your unique potential and unlocking your best self."

LeBron James, Professional Basketball Player

LeBron James, widely regarded as one of the greatest basketball players of all time, is a prime example of someone who has harnessed his talents, strengths, and superpowers to achieve extraordinary success on and off the court.

Talents: LeBron's natural athleticism and basketball IQ were evident from a young age. Born in Akron, Ohio, he was recognized as a basketball prodigy in high school, earning national attention before even entering the NBA. His physical gifts—size, speed, and agility—gave him an edge, but LeBron didn't rely solely on his natural talents.

Strengths: Throughout his career, LeBron has worked tirelessly to develop his skills and adapt his game. He became a versatile player capable of excelling in any position, mastering scoring, defense, and playmaking. His leadership, basketball intelligence, and work ethic made him a complete player who could dominate in all aspects of the game. He also honed his ability to perform under pressure, leading his teams to multiple NBA championships and earning four MVP awards.

Superpowers: LeBron's influence extends beyond basketball to philanthropy, business, and social justice. He used his platform to create the LeBron James Family Foundation, which provides educational opportunities to at-risk youth. His "I PROMISE School" in Akron offers students a pathway to success, demonstrating his commitment to giving back to his community. Additionally, LeBron has become a powerful voice for social change, speaking out on issues of racial inequality and using his platform to advocate for justice.

LeBron's ability to harness his talents, refine his strengths, and leverage his superpowers has made him a global icon. He exemplifies what it means to fully realize one's potential, not just by achieving greatness in a chosen field but by using that success to uplift others and make a lasting impact.

LeBron James' journey showcases how fully unleashing your talents, strengths, and superpowers can lead to exceptional achievements and influence across multiple domains.

Strength-based assessment tools empower individuals to identify their innate talents, focus on what they naturally excel at, and maximize their potential. They provide a clearer path to personal and professional growth by building on what makes each person unique.

Strengths-Based Assessment Tools

Assessing your strengths is not about boasting but acknowledging the unique gifts you bring to the world. It is a journey of self-discovery and empowerment where you uncover the tools you need to thrive.

Strength-based assessments help you to identify and leverage your unique strengths and talents. In contrast to traditional assessments, which focus on weaknesses and areas for improvement, strength-based assessments prioritize identifying and building upon our strengths and positive attributes. By highlighting what you do best and enjoy most, these assessments help you gain self-awareness, boost confidence, and maximize your potential for success. Strength-based assessments can inform talent management strategies in organizational settings, enhance team dynamics, and foster a culture of appreciation and empowerment.

Strength-based assessments contribute to personal and professional growth by recognizing and capitalizing on your strengths, leading to greater engagement, productivity, and fulfillment.

Before using any assessment, it is essential to consider the context, purpose, and ethical considerations. Additionally, interpretations of results are most valuable when guided by trained professionals, such as coaches or psychologists.

StandOut 2.0: Assess Your Strengths, Find Your Edge, Win at Work

StandOut 2.0: Assess Your Strengths, Find Your Edge, Win at Work by Marcus Buckingham is a book that aims to help individuals discover their unique strengths and leverage them for personal and professional success. Buckingham, a well-known author and speaker on strengths-based development, provides insights and tools to help readers maximize their potential.

Overall, *StandOut 2.0* offers you a framework for understanding your unique strengths and actionable insights for using them to achieve personal and professional success. Combining the assessment tool with the book's guidance can enhance your performance and help you find fulfillment in your work.

Now, Discover Your Strengths

Now, Discover Your Strengths is a book by Marcus Buckingham and Donald O. Clifton. The book's central theme is based on the idea that you should focus on developing and using your natural strengths rather than trying to fix your weaknesses. The authors argue that identifying and understanding one's unique strengths is crucial for personal and professional success. The book introduces the StrengthsFinder assessment, a tool developed by the Gallup Organization, which identifies your top five strengths out of a list of thirty-four. Buckingham and Clifton emphasize that by aligning one's work and activities with one's strengths, you can achieve higher performance, satisfaction, and overall well-being.

Do What You Are

Do What You Are is a popular career development book by Paul D. Tieger and Barbara Barron. The book is based on the Myers-Briggs Type Indicator (MBTI), a psychological tool that categorizes individuals and celebrates their unique personality types. The book's central premise is that understanding your personality type can guide you toward a career that aligns with your strengths, preferences, and natural inclinations and respects and values your individuality. Tieger and Barron provide insights into each of the sixteen personality types, offering guidance on potential career paths, work environments, and strategies for success based on your unique personality profile, making you feel understood and unique in your career journey.

The authors argue that you can achieve greater job satisfaction and professional success by aligning career choices with inherent preferences and strengths. The practical advice, real-life examples, and detailed type descriptions make this book a valuable resource for anyone at a career crossroads or looking to enhance their career trajectory.

StrengthsFinder 2.0

StrengthsFinder 2.0 is a book by Tom Rath, based on the StrengthsFinder assessment developed by Gallup. The book is designed to help you identify and leverage your unique strengths for personal and professional development. The StrengthsFinder assessment identifies your top five strengths out of thirty-four, providing insights into their innate talents and capabilities. Rath argues that focusing on strengths rather than weaknesses is the key to success and fulfillment.

The book is structured around maximizing readers' potential by honing their strengths and strategically applying them in their lives. *StrengthsFinder 2.0* includes an access code for readers to take the online StrengthsFinder assessment. It provides detailed descriptions of each of the thirty-four strengths and offers practical advice on applying them for improved performance and satisfaction. The book aims to help you understand, appreciate, and harness your strengths to achieve greater success and well-being.

My Story—Talents, Strengths, and Superpowers

Embarking on this journey to discover my superpowers, talents, and strengths was profound. My transformation is a multi-faceted journey encompassing reading, learning, personal networking, meditation, and cultivating a growth mindset.

I learned that the best leaders and high achievers' habits are learning, which is one of their superpowers. As a result of studying these high-achievers, I began associating and connecting with other high-achieving learners. Reading books and taking courses gave me a wealth of knowledge and perspectives, increasing my self-confidence. As a result, learning became one of my superpowers.

Continuous learning helped me to develop new skills, adapt to change, and unlock my talents and strengths. This enabled me to open doors professionally that would not have been open to me before. Learning helped me to develop the concepts and ideas in this book.

I researched my passions and achievements, received feedback from others, and uncovered qualities that define my capabilities. My values resonated with my authentic self, and I recognized patterns in moments of success and fulfillment. Valuable insights came from compliments and stories from those around me, life experiences, and personal assessments confirming my distinctive abilities.

My networking became a superpower that connected me to like-minded individuals who offered me support, guidance, and opportunities for collaboration and growth. For example, I took the assessment in *Stand-Out 2.0: Assess Your Strengths, Find Your Edge, Win at Work* by Marcus Buckingham. It is a simple-to-use assessment that provides insights into your superpowers, talents, and strengths and where to use them best. As a result, this assessment identified one of my superpowers as Connector, which is the ability to connect to and establish trust-based relationships with a diverse group of people.

Being a connector helped me establish role models/mentors, serve others, and complete projects with competent professionals. I did not have to guess my superpower—Connector. I then could communicate and embrace what value I provided to others and the projects I worked on. I became more mindful and aware of the people I associated with and did my best to avoid toxic people and environments that negatively impacted me. I now associate with people and environments that best suit me.

My meditation helped me cultivate inner peace and clarity and to navigate life's challenges with grace and mindfulness. High performers—Michael Jordan, Shaquille O'Neal, LeBron James, and Navy SEALs—use meditation and mindfulness as a mental strength and stress reduction technique. Meditation and mindfulness calm me down when dealing with uncertainty and challenging situations.

Central to this transformation is a growth mindset, which enabled me to embrace challenges as opportunities for learning and see failure as a stepping stone to success. Together, these practices helped to create a foundation to thrive personally, professionally, and spiritually. This has increased my psychological strength and resilience.

It is not an easy journey, but by adopting a growth mindset and seeking guidance from mentors and role models, I have overcome challenging obstacles and learned from my experiences.

Discovering your talents, strengths, and superpowers is about more than self-awareness; it's about embracing what makes you unique and using those gifts to make a meaningful impact. Your greatest potential lies in aligning who you are with what you do.

Summary

In the journey of self-leadership and discovery, it is essential to identify your talents, strengths, and superpowers. These are not just skills or abilities but unique gifts that set us apart and enable us to make a meaningful impact in the world. You unlock your potential and embark on personal and professional fulfillment. As you harness the power of your superpowers, talents, and strengths, you gain the confidence and courage to face life's challenges, pursue your passions, and effect positive change. Through introspection, exploration, and growth, you uncover the keys to unlocking your true potential and creating a future filled with purpose and possibility.

This introspective journey gives you profound insights into your authentic self. The self-assessment serves as a valuable tool for personal growth, allowing you to identify areas for improvement, leverage your strengths, and align your actions with your values. It is a dynamic process that enhances your self-awareness and empowers you to make informed decisions, set meaningful goals, and cultivate a purposeful and fulfilling life. The self-assessment becomes a compass that guides you toward a deeper understanding of yourself and the path to realizing your true potential.

Strengths-based leadership is an approach that focuses on leveraging and developing your strengths instead of concentrating on weaknesses. This type of leadership promotes a positive and empowering work environment where you are encouraged to excel in areas where you naturally thrive. Strengths-based leadership fosters a culture of continuous learning and growth. You are motivated to build on your strengths while developing new ones. This contributes to your long-term success and assists you in achieving your goals.

Action Steps

Engaging in assessments is a transformative process that invites you to explore the intricacies of your personality, skills, and aspirations. It is a deliberate and structured examination of one's strengths, values, and life goals.

1. Take a moment to review the lists in this chapter. Recognize your talents, strengths, and superpowers. What makes you unique? What superpowers, talents, and strengths can you identify and celebrate? We all have strengths, superpowers, talents, and skills to offer the world.

2. Review the assessment list, get out a notebook, and write down the results of the assessments and your self-discovery.

3. Review the following assessments. Identify careers, your personality type, and styles based on the assessments.

   + *StandOut 2.0: Assess Your Strengths, Find Your Edge, Win at Work*—Marcus Buckingham
   + *Do What You Are*—Paul D. Tieger and Barbara Barron.
   + *StrengthsFinder 2.0*—Tom Rath
   + *Now, Discover Your Strengths*—Marcus Buckingham and Donald O. Clifton

4. Write the results of the assessments down in your notebook.

CHAPTER 3

Goal Setting Tips and Techniques

"The greater danger for most of us lies not in setting our aim too high and falling short, but in setting our aim too low and achieving our mark."

Michelangelo—Italian Sculptor and Painter

Goal Setting

Every outstanding achievement begins with a single step and a heart full of dreams. Remember, the path to success is not a straight line but a winding road filled with challenges and triumphs. Embrace each moment as an opportunity to grow and learn.

Set your goals to reach a destination and embark on a journey of discovery. Let your passions guide you, and trust your ability to overcome obstacles. No matter how small, each step you take brings you closer to the life you envision.

Stay committed to your dreams, and don't be afraid to adjust your course as you learn and evolve. Celebrate every milestone, no matter how minor, for they are the building blocks of your success.

"A very great vision is needed, and the man who has it must follow it as the eagle seeks the deepest blue of the sky."

Chief Crazy Horse—Native American—Lakota Sioux Warrior

Goal Setting Benefits

Creating goals offers numerous benefits that enhance both personal and professional growth. Clear goals provide direction and focus, helping you prioritize your efforts and resources toward what truly matters. They serve as a roadmap, breaking down larger aspirations into manageable steps, making tracking progress and staying motivated easier. Setting goals also increases accountability, as you can measure your achievements against specific benchmarks, fostering a sense of accomplishment as you reach each milestone. Additionally, goals promote discipline and perseverance, encouraging you to push through obstacles and stay committed to your vision. Goal setting empowers you to take control of your life, build confidence, and achieve greater success by turning your dreams into actionable plans.

Benefits of Creating and Setting Goals:

+ **Provides Direction and Focus**: Helps prioritize efforts and resources toward what truly matters.

+ **Offers a Roadmap**: Breaks down larger aspirations into manageable steps.

+ **Enhances Motivation**: It makes tracking progress and staying motivated easier.

+ **Increases Accountability**: Allows measurement of achievements against specific benchmarks.

+ **Fosters a Sense of Accomplishment**: Celebrating milestones boosts confidence.

5. **Promotes Discipline and Perseverance**: Encourages pushing through obstacles and staying committed.

6. **Empowers Personal and Professional Growth**: Helps turn dreams into actionable plans.

7. **Builds Confidence**: Achieving goals strengthens self-belief and resilience.

Creating Goals

Start With Goals: Creating clear goals is crucial. Clear goals provide direction, focus, and motivation.

Steps To Help You Create Goals:

+ **Define Your Purpose:** Defining the purpose behind your goals is crucial. When setting goals, you must consider what you hope to achieve and the underlying reasons driving your desire to achieve them. By clarifying your purpose, you can establish distinct objectives that align with your overall intentions.

+ **Set Specific and Measurable Objectives:** After determining your purpose, it is essential to break it down into measurable objectives. Creating quantifiable goals allows you to track your progress and assess whether you have achieved them.

+ **Prioritize Your Goals:** Prioritizing your goals is essential to efficiently managing your time and resources. It is advisable to prioritize the most significant and achievable objectives and work towards attaining them. This strategy will enable you to optimize your time and resources.

+ **Make Goals Realistic and Attainable:** It is crucial to balance difficulty and achievability. Consider your skills, resources, and available time. Overly ambitious goals may lead to frustration and loss of motivation, while achievable goals can bring a sense of accomplishment and help keep you motivated.

+ **Break Goals Into Smaller Tasks:** Breaking your goals into smaller, more manageable tasks can make them more achievable. This approach can prevent you from feeling overwhelmed and make it easier to tackle each task. Creating a timeline or schedule can also help you stay organized and track your progress as you complete each task.

+ **Write Down Your Goals:** Putting thoughts into writing can help solidify them and be a constant reminder. You can document them in a journal, on a whiteboard, or via productivity apps. Regularly reviewing your goals is crucial for staying focused and motivated.

+ **Evaluate and Adjust as Needed:** It is crucial to regularly assess your progress and make necessary changes to your goals. Stay adaptable and open to adjusting your goals to ensure you remain on the right path.

Remember, clear goals give you a sense of direction and purpose. Setting specific, measurable, realistic, and prioritized goals allows you to stay focused, motivated, and succeed. You have the power to shape your future. With determination, perseverance, and an open heart, there are no limits to what you can achieve. Believe in your journey, and let your dreams illuminate the path ahead.

"Tom Brady's success isn't just a result of talent but a testament to relentless preparation, mental toughness, and the refusal to settle for anything less than greatness."

Tom Brady, NFL Hall of Fame Quarterback, On Achieving Goals

Tom Brady, widely considered one of the greatest quarterbacks in NFL history, often speaks about the dedication and relentless pursuit needed to achieve goals. He emphasizes the importance of setting clear objectives and focusing on the steps required. According to Brady, achieving goals is not just about talent but about consistently showing up, putting in the effort, and staying committed to the process, even when faced with obstacles or setbacks. His career is a testament to the belief that you can overcome challenges and reach the pinnacle of success with perseverance, preparation, and an unwavering mindset.

Brady also underscores the significance of mental conditioning, emphasizing the importance of visualization and staying mentally sharp, particularly in high-pressure situations. His approach highlights that achieving goals is as much about mental resilience as physical ability.

Moreover, Brady attributes much of his success to staying focused on long-term goals without being distracted by short-term failures or successes. Even after reaching the highest levels of his sport, his commitment to continuous improvement is a powerful reminder that achieving goals is an ongoing process. It requires a willingness to adapt, learn from every experience, and persist in adversity. His journey illustrates that true success comes from the relentless pursuit of excellence, a mindset that drives you to push beyond your limits and achieve greatness.

Clear goals are the compass that guides us toward success. When we measure our progress, we turn aspirations into actionable steps, ensuring every effort aligns with our purpose and vision.

Establish SMART Goals and Activities

SMART goals are a framework for setting specific, measurable, achievable, relevant, and time-bound objectives.

The Acronym SMART Stands for the Following:

+ **Specific:** A SMART goal should be clear and well-defined. It should answer the questions of who, what, where, when, why, and how. The goal should be specific and unambiguous, leaving no room for interpretation.

+ **Measurable:** A SMART goal should include specific criteria for measuring progress and determining success. It involves quantifiable or observable metrics that can track the achievement of the goal. This allows for objective evaluation and provides a sense of accomplishment when reaching milestones.

+ **Achievable:** A SMART goal should be realistic and attainable. It should stretch your capabilities and push you outside your comfort zone, but it should still be within the realm of possibility. It considers the resources, skills, and time necessary to accomplish the goal.

+ **Relevant:** A SMART goal should align with your objectives, values, and aspirations. It should be directly relevant and significant to your personal or professional growth. It ensures that your efforts are focused on what truly matters to you and contribute to your larger goals.

+ **Time-bound:** A SMART goal should have a specific time limit or deadline for completion. This creates a sense of urgency, helps prioritize tasks, and allocates resources effectively. Having a defined timeline creates a sense of accountability and motivates action.

Developing SMART goals is essential for effective goal setting. It involves ensuring that your goals are Specific, Measurable, Achievable, Relevant, and Time-bound. By doing this, you create a solid foundation for success. When your objectives are clear, you can create a roadmap for progress and set a deadline for achievement. This empowers you to turn your aspirations into tangible results, one SMART goal at a time.

By setting SMART goals, you can turn your dreams into achievable milestones, your aspirations into tangible actions, and your potential into reality.

Overcoming obstacles is about embracing the lessons hidden within challenges. It's not the barrier that defines you, but the strength and ingenuity you summon to rise above it.

Obstacles In the Way

Embarking on your journey of goal setting is an empowering endeavor that promises professional and personal growth, achievement, and transformation. However, as with any meaningful journey, obstacles can emerge, potentially deterring you from reaching your desired destinations.

In this exploration, you delve into the intricate landscape of your goal setting and shed light on the potential roadblocks that may arise. Prepare for unexpected twists and turns. You must equip yourself with the knowledge and tools to navigate challenges and stay the course.

Unveiling the roadblocks to goal setting invites you to set your sights on the horizon and be aware of the potential obstacles hindering your progress. From the subtle nuances of self-doubt to the external factors that vie for our attention, you will uncover the factors that can cast shadows on our aspirations. Effective goal setting involves more than just defining objectives; it also requires an initiative-taking approach to anticipate challenges and obstacles. This means considering what might go wrong and distracting yourself from your goals. It involves listing how you procrastinate and identifying potentially risky solutions or environments that could hinder your progress. To succeed, it is essential to focus on the depth and dedication required to achieve your goals, not just superficially. Maintaining a daily journal to track procrastination patterns, practicing metacognition to understand your thinking processes, and embracing the concept of "first delay" by accepting external interruptions with patience are all valuable strategies to stay on track and overcome obstacles on your path to achievement.

Obstacles are not roadblocks but stepping stones on the path to greatness. With resilience, determination, and unwavering faith in yourself, every challenge becomes an opportunity for growth and transformation. Embrace the journey; overcoming obstacles means discovering our true strength and potential. Keep moving forward with courage and conviction, knowing that every setback is simply a setup for a comeback. You can overcome anything that stands in your way. Believe in yourself, and you will conquer mountains.

By confronting these challenges head-on, you gain the power to transform obstacles into stepping stones. Throughout this journey, you will explore strategies, insights, and practical advice to fortify your resilience, enhance your determination, and ensure no challenge awaits your dreams.

Common Obstacles When Setting and Pursuing Your Goals:

+ **Lack of Clarity:** Unclear goals can lead you to confusion, making it difficult to determine the necessary steps to achieve them.

+ **Overwhelming Goals:** Setting too ambitious or complex goals can be overwhelming, causing discouragement and a sense of impossibility.

+ **Lack of Direction:** Not knowing how or where to begin can prevent you from acting toward your goals.

+ **Procrastination:** Putting off action on goals due to a lack of motivation, fear of failure, or a tendency to delay tasks.

+ **Lack of Commitment:** When you are not fully committed to your goals, you might abandon them when faced with challenges.

+ **External Distractions:** External factors, such as social media, work demands, or personal issues, can divert your attention from pursuing goals.

+ **Negative Self-Talk:** Negative thoughts and self-doubt can undermine confidence and deter you from pursuing your goals.

+ **Lack of Resources:** Limited access to necessary resources, whether financial, educational, or logistical, can hinder your goal attainment.

+ **Perfectionism:** Striving for perfection can lead you to fear failure and prevent you from taking necessary risks.

+ **Lack of Support:** A lack of encouragement or support from your family, friends, or colleagues can make pursuing your goals challenging.

+ **Time Constraints:** Balancing goal pursuit with other responsibilities and commitments can be difficult, leading to time management challenges.

- **Fear of Failure:** The fear of not achieving a goal or facing setbacks can paralyze you and prevent you from trying.

- **Lack of Accountability:** Without accountability measures, you may lose track of your progress and become less motivated to achieve your goals.

- **Changing Circumstances:** External factors, such as unforeseen events or personal circumstances, can disrupt goal pursuit.

- **Not Celebrating Progress:** Failing to acknowledge and celebrate small wins along the way can lead to burnout and decreased motivation.

- **Comparing to Others:** Constantly comparing progress can lead to feelings of inadequacy and diminish the sense of accomplishment.

- **Unrealistic Expectations:** Setting unrealistic time limits or expectations for goal attainment can lead to disappointment and frustration.

- **Lack of Flexibility:** Being overly rigid with goals can prevent you from adjusting your plans when necessary.

- **Feeling Overburdened:** Trying to pursue too many goals simultaneously can lead you to spread yourself too thin and feel overwhelmed.

- **Past Failures:** Previous failures can create self-doubt and skepticism about setting and pursuing new goals.

Overcoming these obstacles requires a combination of self-awareness, resilience, and effective planning. Challenges are an inevitable part of life; overcoming them makes you stronger and more resilient. By being self-aware of your strengths, weaknesses, and motivations, you can develop an unwavering determination to persist in adversity. Coupled with effective planning and a strategic approach, you can chart a course toward success. Remember, every obstacle can be a stepping stone towards achieving your goals and emerging victorious on the other side.

Obstacles and roadblocks are not barriers;
they are opportunities in disguise. Each challenge
we face sharpens our resolve, deepens our wisdom,
and strengthens our journey toward success.

Overcoming Obstacles and Roadblocks

When achieving your goals, success comes to those who plan strategically and remain resilient in the face of obstacles. Do not let challenges hold you back with the right attitude and approach, you can overcome anything that stands in your way and make your dreams a reality. Remember, every setback is an opportunity to gain experience and grow stronger, so keep pushing forward and never give up on your aspirations.

Strategies to Help You Navigate Challenges and Achieve Your Goals:

+ **Identify Potential Obstacles:** Anticipate potential challenges in achieving your goals. These could include external factors such as time constraints, financial limitations, unexpected setbacks, and internal factors such as self-doubt or fear of failure.

+ **Develop a Flexible Plan:** Create a detailed plan outlining the steps needed to achieve your goals but remain flexible enough to adapt to changing circumstances. Build contingency plans for potential obstacles and be prepared to adjust your approach as needed.

+ **Break Goals into Smaller Tasks:** Break down your larger goals into smaller, manageable tasks or milestones. This makes the overall goal less overwhelming and allows you to focus on progressing one step at a time.

+ **Stay Focused on the Outcome:** Keep your goals in mind and focus on the desired outcome, even when faced with challenges. Visualize yourself achieving your goal and remind yourself why it is important.

- **Seek Support:** Do not be afraid to ask for help or seek support from others when needed. This could include seeking advice from mentors or peers, delegating tasks to others, or finding accountability partners to help keep you on track.

- **Practice Resilience:** Cultivate resilience by effectively developing coping mechanisms to manage stress and setbacks. Learn from failures, bounce back quickly, and use setbacks as opportunities for growth and learning.

- **Stay Committed:** Stay committed to your goals and keep moving forward, even when faced with obstacles or setbacks. Focus on your progress so far and remind yourself why you set the goal in the first place.

- **Celebrate Progress:** Celebrate your achievements and milestones, no matter how small. This helps to maintain motivation and momentum and provides positive reinforcement for your efforts.

By implementing these strategies and maintaining a positive mindset, you can overcome obstacles in goal setting and stay on track to achieve your objectives.

My Story—Writing This Book Goal

Writing a book is a significant undertaking that often involves numerous challenges, from developing ideas to organizing them into a coherent narrative. It requires a steadfast commitment to my vision and the ability to navigate setbacks and adapt my plans when necessary. By cultivating determination and resilience, I maintained my focus and continued moving forward, even when the path became difficult.

Clear, achievable goals gave me a sense of direction and purpose, helping me stay motivated and focused. I started by setting realistic goals and breaking the writing process into manageable tasks—outlining chapters, conducting research, or drafting specific sections. This approach made the book writing project feel less overwhelming and allowed me to track my progress more efficiently, building momentum as I completed each task.

It's natural to encounter challenges such as writer's block, self-doubt, or time constraints, but remember that each obstacle is an opportunity to grow and refine our skills. Obstacles can leave us feeling stuck, while self-doubt can make us question our abilities and the value of our work. Time constraints can add pressure and stress, making maintaining a steady writing routine difficult.

Instead of allowing these obstacles to get in the way, I used them as learning experiences that contributed to my developing a growth and grit mindset. Viewing obstacles as challenges can also push us to develop new strategies and approaches, enhancing our skills and resolve.

Lessons Learned from Writing this Book

Start by setting realistic goals and breaking goals into manageable tasks. Clear, achievable goals can provide direction and purpose, helping us stay motivated and focused. Break down goals into processes and smaller tasks. This approach makes the project feel less overwhelming and allows us to track our progress more easily, building momentum as we complete each task.

Create a consistent schedule to build discipline and momentum and allow us the freedom to achieve tasks imperfectly at first. Establishing a routine helps develop discipline and makes achieving our goals a habitual part of our day. Dedicating specific time to smaller tasks can create a sense of accountability and reduce procrastination. Accomplish smaller tasks without worrying about perfection. This encourages creativity and progress, as we can always revise and polish our work later.

Seek feedback and support from trusted peers to gain perspective and encouragement. Sharing our work with others can provide valuable insights and constructive criticism to enhance your work. Feedback from friends, mentors, or role models can help you identify areas for improvement and offer new perspectives on your ideas. Additionally, having a support system can provide encouragement and motivation, helping us stay committed to our goals.

Embrace setbacks as part of the creative process, learning from them and using them to fuel your progress. Setbacks are inevitable in any creative endeavor but can also be valuable learning experiences. Instead of becoming discouraged, view these challenges as opportunities to grow and refine your approach. Analyze what went wrong and adjust each strategy moving forward. Each obstacle overcome can strengthen our skills and determination, bringing us closer to achieving our goals.

Stay connected to our passion and purposes and visualize our goal's impact. Remembering our why can help us push through tough times. Remind yourself of the message we want to share and the effect we hope our goals will have. Visualizing our work's positive impact can reignite our motivation and inspire us to persevere.

We can navigate obstacles and bring our vision to life with perseverance and a positive mindset. Accomplishing our goals is a journey that requires dedication, resilience, and adaptability. Maintaining a positive outlook and a strong belief in overcoming challenges can transform obstacles into stepping stones toward success. Embrace the journey, learn from each experience, and trust our ability to achieve our goals.

Goal setting is the bridge between dreams and reality. Clear, actionable goals focus your energy, build momentum, and empower you to turn intentions into achievements.

Summary

Goal setting is not just a simple task but a life-changing process that helps you to achieve your aspirations and take control of your destiny. By setting goals, you gain clarity on your objectives, focus energy, and develop a sense of purpose and direction. Goals function as guideposts, showing you the way forward and providing a framework for action and achievement. They inspire motivation and drive, encouraging you to push beyond your limits, overcome obstacles, and strive for excellence.

Action Steps

Achieving goals is not just about reaching a destination; it is about embracing your journey, persevering through challenges, and realizing your potential.

1. Review the goal-setting framework.

    + Write down two to three sub-goals you can accomplish to develop momentum in achieving your goals.
    + Write down your goals, timelines, and resources needed.

2. Check to see that your values align with your goals.

3. Write down obstacles in your way that may hinder your achieving your goals.

    + For each obstacle, write down a solution to overcome the obstacle.
    + Write down what you will learn from overcoming each obstacle.

4. Develop a support network that will assist you in achieving your goals.

5. Celebrate each win, however small, in achieving your goals.

CHAPTER 4

Developing Your Learning Superpower

"Leadership and learning are indispensable to each other."
President John F. Kennedy

Learn and Lead

Greetings, and welcome to the world of learning—a place where curiosity meets growth! Learning is a lifelong journey that unlocks new possibilities, broadens your horizons, and enables you to achieve your full potential.

Embrace the mindset of a lifelong learner, where every experience is an opportunity for growth and discovery. Always remember that cultivating a mindset that values learning requires consistent practice and effort. Nonetheless, by dedicating time and commitment, anyone can form the habits and beliefs that enable them to tackle life with a growth and learning-oriented attitude.

Adopting a learning mindset involves appreciating the journey of learning and personal development and viewing difficulties and roadblocks as chances to improve oneself. Having a learning mindset means valuing the process of learning and growth and perceiving challenges and obstacles as opportunities to develop and enhance oneself. Developing a learning mindset involves cultivating beliefs, attitudes, and behaviors that prioritize and foster continuous learning and personal growth.

Maintaining a habit of learning is crucial. Our busy schedules make it easy to overlook personal and professional growth. Dealing with challenges in the learning process is a natural part of the journey. Let us take a moment to set specific learning goals and prioritize this aspect of our lives. Overcoming learning challenges can be a transformative process that leads to personal growth and academic success. Each challenge conquered is a step towards a more empowered and successful you.

As you embark on your learning journey, be open to new experiences, embrace challenges as opportunities, and never stop seeking knowledge. Remember, learning is not solely about acquiring knowledge. It is about developing critical skills, nurturing a growth mindset, and embracing the joy of discovery. This joy, this thrill of uncovering new knowledge, makes the learning journey so exciting and fulfilling.

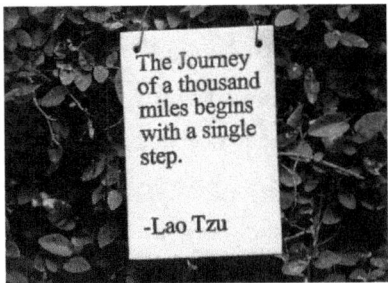

The Journey of a thousand miles begins with a single step.

-Lao Tzu

"The journey of a thousand miles begins with a single step."
Lao Tzu—Chinese Philosopher and Writer

Learning Journey

The learning journey is a path of endless discovery, a quest to unlock the treasures of knowledge and wisdom that lie within. Gaining knowledge and honing skills are crucial for personal and professional growth. Learning is the cornerstone of achieving these goals as it widens your understanding and helps you acquire new competencies and expertise.

Learning is a journey that inspires you to acquire practical and theoretical knowledge in your areas of interest or professional fields. Influential leaders are a testament to this, as they are known for their thirst for knowledge and commitment to continuous learning and personal growth. They actively seek new information, stay updated on industry trends, and invest in honing their skills and expertise.

Influential leaders strongly desire knowledge and prioritize continuous learning and personal growth. They proactively seek new information, keep themselves updated on industry trends, and invest in honing their skills and expertise.

You can, too!

Negative feelings are not signs of failure in learning, but rather signals of growth. Every frustration and setback is a stepping stone to mastering new skills and deepening our understanding.

Characteristics of A Learning Mindset

A learning mindset is characterized by a profound openness to new experiences, a relentless curiosity, and an unwavering commitment to growth. With this mindset, you view challenges as opportunities for growth rather than obstacles to avoid, approaching each new endeavor with excitement and possibility. You possess a deep-seated belief in your ability to learn and adapt, embracing failure as a natural part of the learning process and leveraging setbacks as valuable opportunities for reflection and improvement. Furthermore, with a learning mindset, you actively seek feedback and constructive criticism, recognizing it as a catalyst for growth and self-discovery. You prioritize continuous self-improvement, seeking new knowledge and skills to expand your horizons and reach your full potential. A learning mindset is a state of being and a way of life—an ever-evolving journey toward personal and professional fulfillment.

+ **Self-Awareness:** To enhance your learning experience, it is essential to begin by comprehending your learning style, areas of improvement, and strengths. Understanding your strengths and weaknesses can help you tailor your approach and seek the appropriate guidance.

+ **Set Clear Goals:** By setting clear learning goals and objectives, we can avoid feeling overwhelmed and instead focus on accomplishing smaller, more manageable tasks. Setting specific and achievable goals provides focus and motivation, enabling you to track progress and celebrate successes. Creating well-defined and attainable objectives helps you concentrate and stay motivated. This approach allows you to monitor your progress and achieve success.

+ **Develop Effective Study Techniques:** Discover your unique learning style by trying out various techniques, such as active reading, summarizing, note-taking, mind mapping, using flashcards, and practicing retrieval exercises. By experimenting with different strategies, you can enhance your understanding and engage your mind in exciting ways.

+ **Seek Support and Resources:** It is crucial to seek help when facing obstacles. Various resources, such as teachers, tutors, mentors, study groups, online courses, and educational platforms, are available. Working with others can provide innovative ideas and help you understand the material, so it is essential to ask for help whenever you encounter difficulties or require clarification.

+ **Practice Time Management:** Overcoming learning challenges requires effective time management. It is crucial to schedule consistent and uninterrupted study sessions to establish a productive study routine.

Break your tasks into manageable segments and allocate specific time slots for each. Prioritize essential tasks to avoid procrastination and maximize your study time.

+ **Embrace a Growth Mindset:** Believing in your ability to grow and improve through effort and practice is essential. Instead of fearing challenges, embrace them as chances for personal development and learn from any missteps. Keep a positive attitude towards learning and persist through any obstacles that come your way.

+ **Stay Organized:** A structured approach to managing your learning tasks is crucial. Ensure you systematically organize your learning materials, notes, and resources. You can leverage digital apps, calendars, and to-do lists to stay on top of your assignments, deadlines, and study sessions. Creating a well-structured study environment can minimize distractions and improve your focus.

+ **Practice Self-Care:** It is crucial to prioritize your overall health and wellness. This involves getting enough sleep, consuming nutritious meals, and consistently engaging in physical activity. To manage stress, consider implementing relaxation techniques such as meditation, deep breathing exercises, or hobbies that promote relaxation and rejuvenation.

+ **Embrace Failure as Feedback:** It is important not to let failures or setbacks bring you down. Instead, try to see them as chances to learn and grow. Take the time to analyze what went wrong, pinpoint areas for improvement, and adjust your approach accordingly. You can use your mistakes as stepping stones to achieve success by learning from your mistakes. It is important not to let failures or setbacks bring you down. Instead, try to see them as chances to learn and grow. Take the time to analyze what went wrong, pinpoint areas for improvement, and adjust your approach accordingly. By learning from your mistakes, you can use them as stepping stones to achieve success.

+ **Stay Motivated:** Remember, overcoming learning challenges is a journey that demands patience and persistence. Embrace this process positively, stay committed, and recognize your progress. You can conquer obstacles and reach your full potential with practical methods and support.

By embracing these principles, you can cultivate a learning mindset that enhances your knowledge and skills and contributes to personal and professional development. Remember that learning is a lifelong journey, and adopting a mindset focused on growth and curiosity will serve you well in all aspects of life.

See learning as a superpower you can wholeheartedly adopt as a habit, personally or professionally.

ADVANTAGE

Learning is the gateway to transformation. It doesn't just expand our knowledge; it shifts our perspective, strengthens our resilience, and empowers us to overcome challenges with new insight and wisdom.

Advantages and Benefits of Learning

These advantages and benefits of learning highlight its transformative power in various aspects of life. Whether acquiring knowledge, developing skills, or expanding personal horizons, learning contributes to personal enrichment, professional success, and a fulfilling life.

Learning Advantages and Benefits:

+ **Knowledge and Skill Development:** Learning expands your knowledge base and helps you to acquire new skills and competencies. It equips you with information, theories, and practical abilities in various areas of interest or professional fields. Acquiring knowledge and skills through learning is crucial for personal growth and development. It is fundamental to gaining new competencies and expanding our knowledge base.

+ **Personal Growth:** Learning fosters personal growth and self-improvement. It enhances critical thinking, problem-solving abilities, and decision-making skills. It can also boost your self-confidence, self-awareness, and self-esteem. Improving oneself through learning is essential for personal growth and self-improvement.

+ **Adaptability and Resilience:** Continuous learning enables you to adapt to new situations, technologies, and changes in your personal and professional environments. It enhances resilience by developing your ability to embrace challenges, overcome obstacles, and navigate uncertainty. Continued learning helps you become adaptable and resilient in your personal and professional environments. It allows you to quickly adjust to new situations, technologies, and changes while developing skills to overcome challenges and navigate uncertainty.

+ **Professional Advancement:** Learning is crucial for career development and advancement. Acquiring new knowledge, staying updated with industry trends, and developing new skills can enhance job performance, increase employability, and open doors to new opportunities. To excel in your career, learning must be a top priority. Staying current with industry trends, acquiring new knowledge, and honing your skills can significantly enhance job performance, broaden employment prospects, and unlock new opportunities.

- **Creativity and Innovation:** Learning fuels creativity and fosters innovation. Exposure to innovative ideas, perspectives, and concepts can spark creative thinking, problem-solving, and the generation of innovative solutions. Exposure to innovative ideas, perspectives, and concepts through learning is essential for igniting creativity and promoting innovation. Through this, you can enhance your ability to think creatively and tackle problems efficiently, leading to the development of groundbreaking solutions.

- **Personal Fulfillment:** Learning allows you to pursue your passions, explore new interests, and engage in lifelong learning. It brings a sense of fulfillment, intellectual stimulation, and personal satisfaction. Acquiring knowledge can empower you to fiercely follow your aspirations, explore uncharted territories, and immerse yourself in perpetual learning, resulting in a profound sense of gratification, mental stimulation, and contentment.

- **Improved Communication and Relationships:** Learning can enhance verbal and written communication skills. It facilitates the practical expression of ideas, active listening, and empathy, fostering better relationships and understanding.

- **Cognitive Benefits:** Learning is not just about the here and now. It is an investment in your cognitive health. Learning activities exercise the brain and promote cognitive health, improving memory, concentration, and mental agility. Lifelong learning has been linked to a reduced risk of cognitive decline and improved overall brain function. Studies show that continuous learning can reduce the risk of cognitive decline and improve overall brain function, making it a smart choice for your future.

- **Social Connections and Engagement:** Learning often involves connecting with others with similar interests or goals. It provides opportunities for social interaction, collaboration, and networking, forming meaningful relationships and a sense of community. Making social connections and engaging with others with similar interests or goals is integral to learning. It offers chances for social interaction, collaboration, and networking, which helps form meaningful relationships and a sense of community.

◆ **Personal Empowerment**: Learning empowers you to take control of your growth and development, fostering a sense of independence. It enables you to set and achieve personal goals, make informed decisions, and take charge of your learning journey. Empowerment is an absolute result when it comes to learning. It grants you the power to steer your growth, enabling you to establish and attain your objectives and make educated decisions.

In summary, learning expands horizons and enriches our lives, but it also empowers us to be effective and has a lasting impact on the world. It is a superpower that fuels personal growth, innovation, and positive change.

Begin your journey to develop learning as a superpower!

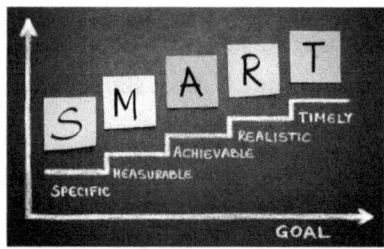

"Intellectual growth should commence at birth and cease only at death."

Albert Einstein

SMART Learning

Establishing SMART learning involves adopting a proactive approach to acquiring knowledge and skills. By setting specific, measurable, achievable, relevant, and time-bound SMART goals, learners can focus on areas that align with their interests and aspirations. It is about leveraging effective strategies and resources to optimize learning and achieve meaningful outcomes. SMART learning emphasizes self-directedness, curiosity, and adaptability, empowering you to take ownership of your learning journey. Additionally, embracing a growth mindset fosters resilience and perseverance in facing challenges, enabling continuous improvement and development.

SMART learning also involves leveraging various learning modalities, such as online courses, books, podcasts, and hands-on experiences, to cultivate a diverse skill set and stay relevant in today's dynamic world. By embracing SMART learning principles, you can unlock your full potential and thrive in personal and professional domains.

The best learning resources challenge our thinking and expand our perspective. True growth comes not from simply gathering information, but from engaging with diverse sources that push us to question, adapt, and innovate.

Learning Resources

+ **Enroll In Local Colleges and Universities.** Enrolling in local growth potentialities can be a fantastic way to continue learning and growing as a leader. By taking advantage of the various programs and courses offered, you can gain new knowledge and skills to help you stay ahead of the curve and make informed decisions that drive your organization forward. Exceptional leaders have found success by always continuing their pursuit of education, so why not join them and see where it takes you?

+ **Go to Your Local Library.** Have you considered visiting your local library? The library is a wonderful place to continue learning and expanding your knowledge base, from books and magazines to online databases and research tools. Plus, it is a free resource you can take advantage of anytime. Why not check it out and see what you can discover?

+ **Take Online Courses.** Online courses are a fantastic way to continue learning and expand your knowledge base. Online education websites offer free, accessible, and affordable courses. My favorite resource for online learning is Coursera.org. You can learn new skills, explore new subjects, and even earn certificates to add to your resume. It is a convenient and flexible way to continue your education and pursue your interests.

+ **Take Advantage of Resources Companies or Organizations May Offer.** Take advantage of your company or organization's resources. This could be anything from professional development programs to mentorship opportunities. It is essential to stay up to date with the latest industry trends and advancements, and your employer may be able to provide you with valuable resources to help you achieve your career goals. Be sure to speak with your supervisor or HR representative to see what options are available to you.

+ **Ask Your Colleagues and Friends.** What are they learning? What are they reading? Hey there! Have you talked to any of our colleagues or friends lately? It might be interesting to hear about what they are learning or reading. It is always good to stay informed and keep up with your industry's latest trends and advancements.

+ **Pay Forward the Learning Resources to Increase Your Network Influence.** We must keep ourselves updated with the latest trends and advancements in our industry. Sharing knowledge with colleagues and friends can increase your network influence.

+ **Develop Role Models and Mentors to Provide You with Insights.** Having role models and mentors to give insights can be incredibly beneficial. They can offer guidance and perspective on our career paths and help us navigate the challenges we may face. Choosing individuals who align with our values and goals and have experience and expertise in our desired field is essential. By learning from their experiences and insights, we can gain valuable knowledge and skills to help us grow personally and professionally. Thank the people who have helped us to become more knowledgeable.

Establishing SMART learning goals is crucial for maximizing personal and professional development. SMART goals are specific, measurable, achievable, relevant, and time-bound, providing a clear roadmap for success. You can focus your efforts and track their progress by setting specific objectives. Measurable goals enable learners to quantify their achievements and stay motivated throughout their journey. Achievable goals ensure that learners set realistic targets that they can feasibly accomplish. Relevant goals are aligned with your interests, values, and long-term aspirations, fostering intrinsic motivation and engagement. Time-bound goals create urgency and help you prioritize your actions effectively. By establishing SMART learning goals, you can harness your potential, overcome challenges, and continuously improve your learning endeavors.

"Thanks to my reading, I have never been caught flat-footed by any situation, never at a loss for how any problem has been addressed before. It doesn't give me all the answers, but it lights what is often a dark path ahead."

General James Mattis—USMC (Ret.)
and former Secretary of Defense

General James Mattis, USMC (Ret.) On Learning and Reading

In *Call Sign Chaos: Learning to Lead*, General James Mattis shares his learning philosophy, which is grounded in the principles of lifelong learning, humility, and self-improvement. His approach is shaped by his experiences as a Marine leader and emphasizes the importance of continuous education to navigate complex leadership challenges.

Key Elements of Mattis's Learning Philosophy:

+ **Lifelong Learning:** Mattis believes learning is a never-ending process, especially for leaders. He stresses that a leader's education should not stop after formal training or schooling. Instead, leaders must continually seek knowledge through reading, observation, and reflection. He states, "You must deliberately plan time to read, think, and reflect." Mattis views reading as an essential way to prepare for a leader's unknown challenges.

+ **Reading as a Strategic Asset:** Mattis is an avid reader and strongly advocates reading history, biographies, and strategic thought. He views books as a way to learn from the experiences of others and avoid repeating mistakes. He often says, "By reading, you learn through others' experiences, generally a better way to do business, especially in our line of work where the consequences of incompetence are so final for young men." Reading is part of a leader's preparation, helping them understand past conflicts, human nature, and strategic principles.

+ **Learning from Mistakes:** A crucial part of Mattis' philosophy is learning from failure. He believes failure provides valuable lessons if leaders reflect on what went wrong and why. He encourages leaders to admit their mistakes and to learn from them without ego getting in the way.

+ **Humility and Curiosity:** Mattis emphasizes the need for humility and a curious mindset. He argues that no leader can know everything and that seeking knowledge from all sources, including subordinates, peers, and mentors, is important. Being humble allows leaders to remain open to learning and improvement. In *Call Sign Chaos*, he says, "If you haven't learned from those who came before you, then you're likely to repeat their mistakes." He consistently highlights that good leaders should never assume they know it all.

+ **Developing Mental Toughness Through Learning:** Mattis views learning as a way to build mental toughness. In military leadership, decisions are often made under extreme stress; having a solid foundation of knowledge and strategic insight provides confidence and clarity. Learning equips leaders with the mental resilience to handle pressure and uncertainty.

+ **Adapting Through Knowledge:** Mattis believes adaptability is crucial to leadership in a rapidly changing world. He stresses that leaders must continually evolve by absorbing new information and perspectives. According to Mattis, this adaptability comes from a constant learning habit.

In summary, General Mattis' learning philosophy in *Call Sign Chaos* revolves around the idea that a leader's effectiveness is directly tied to their commitment to continuous learning. Through reading, reflecting, admitting mistakes, and maintaining curiosity, leaders can develop the strategic insight, resilience, and adaptability required to succeed in complex environments.

Obstacles and Barriers to Effective Learning

Learning can present various challenges for anyone. You may face challenges that could hinder your progress during the learning process. These obstacles may differ based on circumstances, the subject matter, and the learning environment. However, by anticipating these barriers, you can devise effective strategies to overcome them.

Common Obstacles That You May Encounter:

- **Lack of Motivation:** Lack of motivation can hinder learning. When sufficiently engaged and interested in the subject matter, you may need help maintaining focus and making the necessary effort to learn effectively. Lacking motivation can negatively impact your learning ability. With sufficient engagement or interest in the subject matter, maintaining focus and making the necessary effort to learn effectively can become challenging.

- **Lack of Time:** Busy schedules and competing priorities can make finding dedicated time for learning challenging. Balancing work, personal commitments, and other responsibilities can limit the time for focused learning activities.

+ **Distractions:** External distractions, such as noise, technology, or interruptions, can disrupt concentration and hinder effective learning. Internal distractions, such as wandering thoughts or worries, can also detract from the ability to focus and retain information.

+ **Learning Style Mismatch:** Individuals have different learning styles and preferences. If the learning methods and materials do not align with your preferred style (e.g., visual, auditory, kinesthetic), it can impede comprehension and retention of information. Everyone has their unique learning style and preference. When the methods and materials used for learning do not match your preferred style, such as visual, auditory, or kinesthetic, it can hinder your ability to understand and remember the information.

+ **Limited Resources or Access:** Inadequate access to learning resources, such as books, educational materials, or technology, can create barriers to effective learning. Limited access to educational opportunities or institutions can also hinder learning opportunities. A lack of resources or access can hinder effective learning. This includes limited access to learning materials like books, educational resources, or technology. Additionally, limited access to educational institutions or opportunities can impede your learning ability.

+ **Fear of Failure or Judgment:** Fear of failure or concern about being judged by others can create anxiety and inhibit learning. The fear of making mistakes or appearing incompetent may prevent you from taking risks and fully engaging in learning.

+ **Lack of Confidence:** Low self-confidence or self-doubt can undermine learning. Feeling incapable or not believing in one's abilities can hinder motivation, engagement, and the willingness to explore and take on challenges. Lack of confidence can negatively impact learning by causing self-doubt and a belief in one's incapability. Feeling uncertain and lacking faith in their abilities can reduce motivation, engagement, and openness to new challenges.

- **Learning Disabilities or Cognitive Challenges:** Individuals with specific learning disabilities or cognitive challenges may face additional obstacles in the learning process. These challenges may require specialized interventions, accommodations, or support to overcome.

- **Ineffective Study Strategies:** Using effective or efficient study strategies can limit learning progress. Knowing how to manage time effectively, take effective notes, or utilize active learning techniques can help with comprehension, retention, and application of knowledge. Proficiency in time management, note-taking, and active learning is vital in comprehending, retaining, and utilizing information effectively.

- **Limiting Learning Progress with Ineffective Study Strategies:** Utilizing effective or efficient methods for studying can help progress. It is important to manage time effectively, take good notes, or employ active learning techniques to ensure comprehension, retention, and application of knowledge. If you need help with time management, taking practical notes, or using efficient learning methods, you may experience difficulties processing, retaining, and applying new information.

- **Lack of Support or Guidance:** Teacher, mentor, or peer support can help learning. A lack of guidance, feedback, or mentorship can make navigating complex subjects or overcoming obstacles difficult. Not receiving adequate support or guidance from your teachers, mentors, or peers can impede learning progress. Navigating complicated topics or overcoming obstacles can become challenging without proper guidance, feedback, or mentorship.

In summary, learning obstacles can impact everyone negatively. Expect that there will be challenges and obstacles to developing a learning mindset. When we expect challenges and obstacles, we can develop strategies and tactics to overcome them. For example, the cost of education can be expensive; at the same time, resources, i.e., online courses, the library, and community colleges, can significantly reduce traditional education institutions' prices and monetary expenses.

Overcoming Obstacles with a Growth and Learning Mindset

Overcoming obstacles with a growth and learning mindset is not just about surmounting challenges; it is about transforming adversity into opportunity and setbacks into stepping stones for growth. With this mindset, approach obstacles resiliently, viewing them as valuable learning experiences rather than insurmountable barriers. You understand that failure does not reflect your abilities but is a natural part of learning. Instead of becoming discouraged by setbacks, embrace them as opportunities to reflect, learn, and adapt.

With each challenge, you cultivate a deeper understanding of yourself and your capabilities, honing your skills and expanding your knowledge base. By maintaining a positive outlook and a steadfast commitment to growth, you can navigate even the most daunting obstacles with grace and determination, emerging stronger and more resilient on the other side. To accomplish success, it is crucial to comprehend the essential aspects of a growth and learning mindset.

Remember These Key Elements:

+ **Focus On Growth:** A learning mindset involves valuing growth and seeing mistakes and failures as opportunities to gain experience and improve. Focusing on growth means having a learning mindset that values personal development and views mistakes and failures as chances to learn and better oneself.

+ **Curiosity and Thirst for Knowledge:** A learning mindset involves learning about the world and learning new things. It means seeking further information and experiences and being open to new perspectives. Embracing growth requires a curious and open mindset, always seeking new knowledge and perspectives.

- **Willingness to Take Risks:** A learning mindset involves being willing to take risks and try new things, even if it means making mistakes or facing failure. Being open to taking risks and trying new things, even if it means making mistakes or facing failure, is a crucial aspect of having a learning mindset.

- **Belief In the Ability to Learn:** A learning mindset involves having confidence in one's ability to learn and grow and seeing setbacks as temporary rather than permanent. Believing in your ability to acquire new knowledge and skills while perceiving challenges as temporary hurdles rather than permanent barriers constitutes the bedrock of a growth-oriented mindset.

- **Focus on Process:** A learning mindset involves valuing the learning process rather than just the result. It means being patient and persistent when facing challenges and seeing the value in putting in effort and hard work. Developing a learning mindset requires more than focusing on the result. It demands unwavering patience and persistence in overcoming obstacles, acknowledging the significance of exerting effort and work.

Do not be intimidated by obstacles. We all have them. The challenge is to reframe them and use them as learning opportunities.

My Story—Developing A Learning Mindset

My journey in developing a learning mindset took a lot of work. I was a B-plus student in formal schooling and earned an MBA from Temple University. While I was an average student, a significant turning point occurred in 2010 when learning became a critical habit for me. That year,

I experienced personal, professional, and psychological burnout. I found myself financially broke, and my business had failed. Frustrated and stuck, I was fortunate to encounter several events that began my transition and transformation into adopting a learning mindset.

One pivotal event changed my life for the better. In 2010, I was befriended by Colonel John Church, USMC (Ret.), who attended the same gym as I did. He was deployed to Afghanistan in January 2010. I did not know his background, but I eventually discovered that learning was one of his superpowers.

When he returned from a deployment in Afghanistan, he invited me to his office. He was a college professor at a local university. When I entered his office, I was struck by his extensive collection of over one hundred books, an expected sight for a college professor. The first book he showed me was *The Power of Communication* by Helio Fred Garcia. The book had writing all over it, and I could tell he read it well. He suggested I read it. I did. In addition, he assigned me various books to read as part of my homework. The first books he suggested were *Making the Corps* by Tom Ricks, *A Chance in Hell* by Jim Michaels, and *A Soldier's Dream* by William Doyle. Capt. Travis Patriquin, one of the key characters in *A Soldier's Dream*, was known for his exceptional learning abilities. From John's perspective, the lesson was clear: to become a leader, one must be committed to continuous learning, as it equates to having a superpower.

As a follow-up, I studied accomplished professionals—such as athletes, coaches, musicians, business executives, and subject matter experts on learning—to understand the importance of a learning mindset—the one habit I consistently observed among successful people. Successful leaders like Capt. Patriquin and Col. Church are engaged in learning with a growth mindset. They develop and embrace learning as a superpower.

As a result, I cultivated a learning habit by observing role models, taking online courses, reading books, and visiting the library. Becoming an avid learner increased my self-confidence and helped me tackle my challenges. Over time, learning became not just a habit but a personal strength. Learning truly became my superpower!

Remember to approach your challenges with a mindset focused on learning. Develop learning as a superpower! You got this!

Summary

Cultivating a learning mindset is a transformative journey involving curiosity, resilience, and a commitment to continuous improvement. Developing a learning mindset recognizes challenges as opportunities for growth, viewing learning as integral to personal and professional development. By valuing the journey of acquiring new knowledge and skills with a learning mindset, you stay open-minded, seek diverse learning methods, and welcome constructive feedback. Setting learning goals, staying persistent in the face of obstacles, and connecting with a community of learners are all vital components of this mindset. A learning mindset fosters adaptability, enhances problem-solving skills, and empowers you to navigate the complexities of life with a sense of purpose and a commitment to lifelong learning.

Action Steps

1. Develop a habit of learning that can lead to achieving your professional and personal goals.

2. Review the learning resources listed in this chapter. Pick out the resources that you can utilize to achieve your goals.

3. Develop and engage role models and mentors to assist you in your journey.

4. Ignite your potential by daring to dream, persevering through challenges, and embracing your unique strengths.

5. Develop SMART learning goals that augment your professional and personal lives.

CHAPTER 5

Personal SWOT Analysis—
Your Strategic Tool for Success

"Knowing yourself is the beginning of all wisdom."

Albert Einstein

Personal SWOT Analysis Definition

A personal SWOT (strengths, weaknesses, opportunities, threats) analysis aims to understand yourself internally and externally comprehensively. By identifying your strengths and weaknesses, you can focus on leveraging your advantages and addressing areas for improvement. Recognizing opportunities allows you to capitalize on favorable circumstances while acknowledging threats, which helps develop strategies to mitigate potential risks.

The process typically involves reflecting on your personal and professional experiences, skills, values, and aspirations. It is a valuable personal development, career planning, and decision-making tool. Conducting a Personal SWOT Analysis can provide insights that guide you in making informed choices about your education, career paths, and personal growth strategies.

SWOT:

+ **Strengths:** Identifying your strengths is crucial to achieving personal and professional success. Strengths are internal factors that contribute to your growth and development. They include your unique skills, knowledge, experience, and personal characteristics that distinguish you from others. Recognizing and building upon your strengths to maximize your potential and achieve your goals is essential.

+ **Weaknesses:** When assessing your personal and professional growth, it is essential to consider your strengths and weaknesses. While your strengths are unique skills, knowledge, experience, and personal characteristics that contribute to your success, your weaknesses represent areas where you may have limitations or need to improve. You can maximize your potential and achieve your goals by recognizing and working on both.

+ **Opportunities:** When working on your personal and professional growth, it is important to remember the opportunities that are available to you. These external factors can work in your favor and help you achieve your goals. By being aware of these opportunities and leveraging them to your advantage, you can maximize your potential and take your success to the next level.

+ **Threats:** It is essential to be aware of any potential threats that could hinder your progress or pose challenges to achieving your goals. These could be changes in the external environment, competition, or obstacles you must overcome. By being prepared and taking proactive steps to mitigate these threats, you can stay on track and continue progressing towards your personal and professional growth. Remember to stay focused on your goals and not let external factors hold you back from achieving success. Threats are external factors that could hinder your progress or pose challenges to achieving your goals. These could be changes in the external environment, competition, or obstacles you must overcome.

Conducting a personal SWOT analysis allows you to turn self-awareness into action, guiding you to leverage your strengths, address your weaknesses, seize opportunities, and mitigate threats. It's about knowing yourself and strategically crafting your path forward.

Conducting A Personal SWOT Analysis

Conducting a SWOT analysis is like spotlighting your strengths, weaknesses, opportunities, and threats and illuminating the path to your success.

To conduct a personal SWOT analysis, you can use the following steps:

+ **Identify your goal(s):** This is the specific objective you want to achieve, such as finding a new job, starting a business, or learning a new skill.

+ **List your strengths:** Think of all your positive qualities and abilities to help you accomplish your goal. Be honest and realistic; use examples and evidence to support your claims.

+ **List your weaknesses:** Think of all the negative aspects and shortcomings hindering your progress toward your goal. Just like before, be honest and realistic, using examples and evidence to support your claims.

+ **List your opportunities:** Consider all the external factors and situations that can provide advantages and benefits for achieving your goal. Be optimistic and proactive. Again, use examples and evidence to support your claims.

+   **List your threats**: Consider all the external factors and situations that can create obstacles and difficulties in achieving your goal. Be realistic and cautious.

+   **Analyze and prioritize**: Compare and contrast your strengths, weaknesses, opportunities, and threats, and identify the most important and relevant ones for your goal. You can use a matrix or a table to organize and visualize your findings.

+   **Create an action plan**: Based on your analysis, develop a strategy and timeline for achieving your goal.

Developing a personal SWOT analysis can help you gain clarity, set achievable goals, and make informed decisions aligned with your strengths, values, and aspirations. This analysis serves as a personal and professional development roadmap, guiding you toward greater self-awareness, growth, and success.

"If you can't fly then run, if you can't run then walk, if you can't walk then crawl, but whatever you do you have to keep moving forward."

Martin Luther King, Jr.

What Are Your Strengths?

Personal strengths are positive qualities, attributes, or characteristics you possess and can leverage to your advantage in various aspects of life. These strengths are crucial in shaping your personality, behavior, and interactions with others. Identifying and understanding your strengths can help you build self-confidence, achieve goals, and navigate challenges effectively.

Personal Strengths:

- **Creativity:** Thinking outside the box, developing innovative ideas, and approaching problems from different angles.

- **Leadership:** The capacity to guide and inspire others, make decisions, and take responsibility for outcomes.

- **Communication skills:** Effective verbal and written communication, active listening, and expressing ideas clearly.

- **Emotional intelligence:** Being aware of others, managing emotions, and building meaningful relationships.

- **Adaptability:** The capacity to adjust to change, handle uncertainty, and remain flexible in challenging situations.

- **Problem-solving:** The ability to analyze issues, identify solutions, and make well-informed decisions.

- **Resilience:** The ability to bounce back from setbacks, cope with adversity, and maintain a positive outlook.

- **Time management:** Efficiently organize and prioritize tasks to maximize productivity.

- **Empathy:** The capacity to understand and share the feelings of others, showing compassion and support.

- **Optimism:** A positive outlook and the belief that favorable outcomes are possible.

- **Self-discipline:** The ability to stay focused, set and achieve goals, and follow through with commitments.

+ **Teamwork:** The skill to collaborate effectively, value diverse perspectives, and contribute to group efforts.

+ **Humor:** The ability to find and appreciate humor in various situations, promoting a positive atmosphere.

+ **Honesty:** Being truthful and maintaining integrity in interactions with oneself and others.

+ **Analytical Thinking:** The capability to break down complex problems into manageable components and evaluate information critically.

Remember that personal strengths can vary among individuals, and it is essential to recognize and embrace your unique strengths. Building upon and using these strengths can enhance your overall well-being and contribute to personal and professional success. Knowing your strengths can also guide your career and personal choices, help you navigate challenges, and improve your relationships with others.

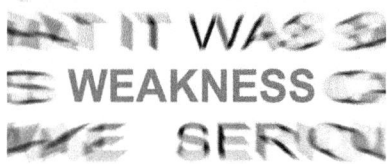

Understanding our weaknesses is a powerful act of self-awareness. It's not about dwelling on what holds us back but recognizing where growth begins, and strength can be forged.

What Are Your Weaknesses?

Personal weaknesses are areas where we may have limitations, challenges, or vulnerabilities. These weaknesses can impact various aspects of our lives and may hinder personal growth, relationships, or professional development. Recognizing and acknowledging our weaknesses is essential for self-awareness and personal improvement.

Personal Weaknesses:

+ **Procrastination:** Delaying or avoiding tasks reduces productivity and increases stress.

+ **Lack of assertiveness:** Difficulty expressing opinions or standing up for oneself can affect personal boundaries and relationships.

+ **Impatience:** Being easily frustrated or unable to wait for desired outcomes.

+ **Poor time management:** Struggling to prioritize tasks effectively or meet deadlines consistently.

+ **Low self-confidence:** A lack of belief in your abilities or worth can hinder you from pursuing goals.

+ **Difficulty with public speaking:** Feeling anxious or uncomfortable when speaking in front of groups.

+ **Inflexibility:** Resisting change or being unwilling to adapt to new situations.

+ **Difficulty with conflict resolution:** Struggling to manage conflicts constructively, leading to strained relationships.

+ **Perfectionism:** Having excessively high standards may make you overly critical of yourself or others.

+ **Tendency to avoid confrontation:** Avoid difficult conversations or necessary confrontations.

+ **Overthinking:** Overanalyzing situations and becoming paralyzed by excessive thoughts.

+ **Problems with attention to detail:** Missing essential details or making careless mistakes.

+ **Lack of organization:** Difficulty keeping track of tasks, possessions, or schedules.

+ **Over-reliance on others' opinions:** Being heavily influenced by external validation or seeking constant approval.

+ **Difficulty saying 'no':** Having trouble setting boundaries and taking on too many commitments.

It is important to remember that our weaknesses are areas for our growth and development, not indicators of personal failure. By recognizing our weaknesses, we can take steps to address them, seek support, or develop strategies to overcome these challenges. Moreover, we can complement our weaknesses with our strengths and seek help from others who excel in those areas, fostering collaboration and mutual support. Embracing self-improvement and working on weaknesses can lead to personal growth and increased self-confidence.

What Are Your Opportunities?

Personal opportunities are external factors or situations that you can take advantage of to achieve your goals, enhance your well-being, and foster personal growth and development. These opportunities can arise from various sources and may present themselves in different areas of your life. Identifying and seizing these opportunities can lead to positive outcomes and progress.

Personal Opportunities:

+ **Educational opportunities:** Access to scholarships, workshops, or training programs that can enhance your knowledge and skills.

+ **Career advancement:** Openings for promotions, new job prospects, or networking events that can lead you to professional growth.

+ **Networking events:** Opportunities to meet and connect with influential or like-minded individuals in your field or area of interest.

+ **Travel and cultural experiences:** Opportunities to travel, study abroad, or engage with diverse cultures, broadening your perspective.

+ **Personal development programs:** Active participation in coaching, mentoring, or self-improvement courses.

+ **Volunteering and community involvement:** Opportunities to give back to the community, have a positive impact, and build meaningful connections.

+ **Extracurricular activities:** Engaging in hobbies, sports, or artistic pursuits that can provide personal fulfillment and relaxation.

+ **Entrepreneurial ventures:** Opportunities to start a business or participate in entrepreneurial initiatives.

+ **Social opportunities:** Events or gatherings that allow you to meet new people and expand your social circle.

+ **Financial opportunities:** Investment prospects or chances to improve one's financial situation.

+ **Technology advancements:** Access to new tools and technologies that can streamline tasks or improve productivity.

+ **Health and wellness opportunities:** Resources for physical and mental well-being, such as fitness classes, counseling services, or healthy lifestyle programs.

- **Public speaking engagements:** Opportunities to present ideas or share expertise in public forums.

- **Leadership roles:** Chances to take leadership positions in organizations, clubs, or community groups.

- **Career transitions:** Opportunities to switch careers and explore different professional paths.

Recognizing personal opportunities requires being initiative-taking, open-minded, and receptive to new possibilities. It is essential to stay informed, network, and maintain a positive attitude to maximize these opportunities. Embracing your opportunities can lead to personal fulfillment, growth, and achieving personal and professional aspirations.

"If you know the enemy and know yourself, you need not fear the result of a hundred battles."

Sun Tzu—Author—The Art of War

What Are Your Threats?

Personal threats are external factors or challenges that can negatively affect our well-being, goals, or overall life satisfaction. These threats can come from various sources and may present risks or obstacles that we need to address to protect our interests and achieve our objectives. Recognizing and understanding personal threats is essential for maintaining safety and making informed decisions.

Personal Threats:

+ **Health Issues:** Sudden illnesses, chronic conditions, or accidents affecting physical and mental well-being.

+ **Financial Challenges:** Job loss, economic downturns, or unexpected expenses that may lead to financial instability.

+ **Relationship Conflicts:** Strained relationships with family members, friends, or partners that can cause emotional distress.

+ **Workplace Stress:** High-pressure work environments, difficult colleagues, or job insecurity.

+ **Personal Safety Concerns:** Living in areas with high crime rates or facing potential dangers while traveling.

+ **Natural Disasters:** In regions prone to earthquakes, hurricanes, floods, or wildfires.

+ **Cybersecurity Threats:** Identity theft, online scams, or privacy breaches.

+ **Addiction or Substance Abuse:** Struggling with addiction issues can severely affect your health and relationships.

+ **Lack of Work-Life Balance:** Overworking and neglecting your personal life can lead to burnout and diminished well-being.

+ **Negative Social Influences:** Being surrounded by individuals who encourage harmful behaviors or undermine your personal growth.

+ **Changing Technology or Job Automation:** Facing job displacement due to technological advancements.

+ **Mental Health Challenges:** Dealing with anxiety, depression, or other psychological issues that impact your daily functioning.

+ **Lack of Support Systems:** Feeling isolated or needing a strong social support network.

- **Personal Biases or Discrimination:** Experiencing discrimination based on factors such as race, gender, religion, or sexual orientation.

- **Environmental Factors:** Living in areas with pollution or hazardous conditions can affect health.

Addressing personal threats involves being proactive, seeking support, and developing strategies to mitigate potential risks. Maintaining physical and emotional well-being, managing finances prudently, building a strong support network, and being aware of personal safety measures are ways to protect yourself from threats. Seeking professional help or advice in challenging situations can also be beneficial. Acknowledging and addressing personal threats can minimize their impact and create a safer and more secure environment for yourself and your loved ones.

True greatness comes from knowing your strengths and weaknesses. Caitlin Clark's journey is a testament to this—she leverages her strengths to shine and confronts her weaknesses to grow, embodying the essence of self-leadership.

Caitlin Clark—College and Professional Basketball Player

Caitlin Clark, the standout basketball player, understands the importance of knowing her strengths and weaknesses like few others. With an astute awareness of her capabilities on the court, she harnesses her strengths, such as her remarkable shooting accuracy, court vision, and leadership, to propel her team to victory. Yet, what sets Caitlin apart is her willingness to confront her weaknesses head-on, transforming them into opportunities for growth. Whether refining her defense, enhancing her conditioning, or fine-tuning her decision-making under pressure, Caitlin embraces the challenge with fierce determination. By understanding her strengths and weaknesses, Caitlin exemplifies the essence of self-awareness and continuous improvement, setting the stage for a legacy of resilience, excellence, and unwavering commitment to becoming the best athlete and person.

"Action is the foundational key to all success."
Pablo Picasso—Spanish Artist and Sculptor

Leverage Insights from Your SWOT Analysis

Leveraging insights from a SWOT analysis helps you make informed decisions, optimize performance, and drive sustainable success by identifying strengths, weaknesses, opportunities, and threats. This helps align resources with overarching objectives and adapt to evolving market dynamics.

Once you have conducted a personal SWOT analysis (strengths, weaknesses, opportunities, and threats), here are steps you can take to leverage the insights gained:

- **Capitalizing on Strengths:** To achieve your goals, leverage your strengths and focus on areas where you excel. This is the key to maximizing your potential and achieving success.

- **Addressing Weaknesses:** Develop strategies to address weaknesses. Seek learning opportunities, feedback, and mentorship, and outsource non-strength tasks in which you do not excel.

+ **Exploring Opportunities:** Evaluate the opportunities identified in your analysis and develop action plans to capitalize on them. This might involve setting specific goals, networking with relevant contacts, or pursuing further education or training.

+ **Mitigating Threats:** It is important to identify potential obstacles that could hinder personal or professional success and develop strategies to address them. This may involve building resilience, creating contingency plans, or proactively tackling challenges before they become major issues.

+ **Creating a Personal Development Plan:** After conducting a SWOT analysis, create a personal development plan by setting specific and achievable goals based on your strengths and opportunities and determine the necessary steps to accomplish them.

+ **Regular Review and Adjustment:** It is essential to regularly review and update your SWOT analysis and personal development plan to track your progress and make necessary adjustments. As your circumstances change, new opportunities and threats can emerge, requiring you to revisit and modify your plan accordingly.

Conducting a personal SWOT analysis can effectively utilize it as a tool for your personal and professional growth. This will help you capitalize on your strengths, overcome weaknesses, and pursue opportunities aligning with your goals and values.

My Story on SWOT Analysis

Developing a SWOT analysis is a powerful tool for my personal growth, especially when navigating the complexities of life, such as experiencing setbacks. This reflective process allowed me to assess my strengths, weaknesses, opportunities, and threats in a structured way, guiding me toward more informed decisions and a stronger sense of self-awareness.

Utilizing The *Do What You Are* book approach, aligned with the Myers-Briggs assessment insights, provided me with an excellent assessment and report that determines and verifies my personality type. This book and assessment led me through the step-by-step process of selecting and verifying my Personality Type. Then, I learned which occupations are popular with each type, discovered helpful case studies, and got a full rundown of my type's work-related strengths and weaknesses.

Based on the assessment and the book, my personality profiles identified me as an ENTJ—Extrovert, Intuitive, Thinking, and Judging. The Myers-Briggs Type Indicator (MBTI) assessment, particularly for individuals identifying as ENTJ, provides valuable insights into my strengths and decision-making styles.

Summary Results of the Assessment—*Do What You Are* and *Myers-Briggs* Assessments:

ENTJ Summary From—*Do What You Are*

ENTJs are known for their decisiveness, driven by a strong preference for momentum and accomplishment. They excel at gathering information and using it to construct creative, strategic visions, often seeing the big picture with clarity. However, what truly sets ENTJs apart is their ability to swiftly transition from planning to execution. They rarely hesitate once a decision is made, preferring action and results over prolonged deliberation. This combination of vision, decisiveness, and a bias for action makes ENTJs natural leaders who thrive in environments that require strategic thinking and a proactive approach to problem-solving.

ENTJ Strengths:

- Ability to see possibilities and implications
- Aptitude for creative problem-solving and examining issues objectively
- Understand complex issues
- Drive and ambition to succeed
- Strong motivation to be competent and excel
- High standards and work ethic
- Create systems and models to achieve objectives

+ Courage to take bold steps
+ Logical and analytical decision-making
+ Decidedness and strong organizational skills
+ Comfort with technology—quick learner

ENTJ Weakness:

+ Impatience with others
+ Brusqueness and lack of tact and diplomacy
+ Tendency to make hasty decisions
+ Lack of interest in mundane details
+ Want to improve something that does not need improving
+ Tendency to overpower others
+ Tendency to not appreciate and praise employees, colleagues, and others
+ Over-emphasizing work life to home life

ENTJ Opportunities:

+ Entrepreneurship: Business Owner, Start-Up Founder
+ Strategic Planning: Strategic Consultant, Analyst
+ Law and Politics: Lawyer, Politician
+ Finance: Investment Banker, Financial Planner
+ Engineering Management: Project Manager, Engineering Director
+ Consulting: Management Consultant
+ Marketing and Advertising: Marketing Director, Brand Strategist
+ Military Leadership: Officer, Commander
+ Education Administration: Dean, Educational Administrator

ENTJ Threats: Understanding these can help ENTJs navigate their careers more effectively.

Short List of Career Threats for ENTJs:

- Overconfidence and Impulsiveness: This may lead to hasty decisions
- Conflict with Authority: Strong opinions can clash with superiors
- Burnout from Overwork: Driven nature risks overexertion
- Difficulty in Delegation: Reluctance to delegate can cause inefficiency
- Inflexibility to Change: Preference for structure may hinder adaptability
- Perceived as Intimidating: Direct style may alienate others
- Overlooking the Human Element: Focus on goals may neglect team morale

Developing a SWOT analysis is a powerful tool for my personal growth, especially when navigating life's complexities, such as experiencing setbacks. This reflective process allowed me to assess my SWOTs in a structured way, guiding me toward more informed decisions and a stronger sense of self-awareness.

Understanding your SWOT—strengths, weaknesses, opportunities, and threats—provides a clear roadmap for growth. It allows you to leverage your strengths, address your weaknesses, seize opportunities, and mitigate threats, empowering you to confidently achieve your goals.

Summary

Utilizing various resources in a Personal SWOT Analysis, such as assessments, self-evaluation, coaching, and counseling, is essential for personal and professional growth. Assessments provide objective data that helps you identify strengths and areas for improvement, offering a clear foundation for development. Self-evaluation complements this by encouraging introspection, allowing you to reflect on your experiences, set goals, and take ownership of your growth journey. Coaching brings an external perspective, offering guidance, accountability, and support in achieving specific goals through structured sessions. Meanwhile, counseling addresses emotional and psychological challenges, helping you overcome barriers to success and well-being. Together, these resources create a comprehensive approach to development, enabling you to achieve your full potential by combining external insights with personal reflection and emotional resilience.

> "In understanding yourself, you unlock
> the path to growth and success!"

Action Plan

1. Develop a written SWOT Analysis to understand your strengths, weaknesses, opportunities, and threats.

2. Utilize assessments to discover your best superpowers, strengths, and talents.

3. Get feedback from trusted mentors, coaches, or friends.

4. Don't let the threats and obstacles get in your way. Develop strategies and techniques to overcome the threats and obstacles you may face.

5. Creating an action plan for a personal SWOT (Strengths, Weaknesses, Opportunities, Threats) analysis involves ensuring that the insights gained are translated into effective personal growth and career development.

CHAPTER 6

Developing A Growth and Grit Mindset

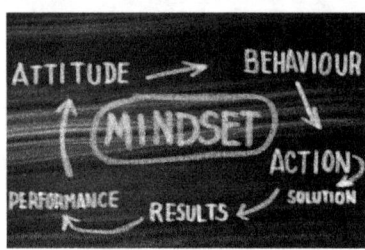

"Attitude is a little thing that makes a big difference."
Winston Churchill—Prime Minister of England

Developing a Growth and Grit Mindset

In today's fast-paced world, the transformative power of a growth and grit mindset is crucial for achieving your personal and professional success. These mindsets are not just ideas; they are catalysts for change. They are based on the belief that our skills and intelligence can be enhanced through hard work, determination, and a readiness to tackle challenges. They empower you to confront obstacles confidently, persist through setbacks, and strive for progress, instilling a sense of confidence and capability.

Embracing a growth and grit mindset can significantly enhance personal and professional development. This mindset equips you with the skills to adapt to new situations, devise innovative solutions, and conquer personal and professional challenges. It instills a strong work ethic, a drive for continuous improvement, and the resilience to bounce back from setbacks.

A growth mindset means recognizing that your talents and abilities are not set in stone and can be developed through learning and practice. With a growth mindset, you see failures as opportunities for growth and welcome challenges as chances to enhance your skills and knowledge. You actively seek feedback, persist through difficulties, and strongly desire to learn and improve continuously, leading to a sense of achievement and inspiration.

A grit mindset is characterized by traits such as determination, passion, and perseverance in the pursuit of long-term goals. It involves the ability to bounce back from setbacks, stay committed to your objectives, and consistently exert effort despite challenges and distractions. A grit mindset is the key to success when achieving greatness, which often requires endurance, patience, and a readiness to overcome obstacles, giving you a sense of purpose and a laser-like focus on your long-term goals.

The growth and grit mindsets are not separate entities but closely connected and work well together. Adopting a growth mindset encourages persistence and effort toward progress, which, in turn, helps develop grit. On the other hand, cultivating grit allows you to maintain your growth mindset by keeping you dedicated to your learning and development journey. This integration of mindsets brings balance and harmony to your personal and professional life.

In our ever-changing and intricate world, developing a mindset of growth and resilience can be genuinely life changing. It enables you to confront challenges bravely, gain valuable insights from setbacks, and persevere in pursuing your aspirations. By embracing these mindsets, you can tap into your fullest potential, embrace continual learning, and successfully navigate the constantly shifting terrain with unwavering strength and resolve, feeling accomplished and motivated by the progress you make.

Developing a growth and grit mindset is about embracing your challenges as opportunities for growth and persisting in adversity. By cultivating resilience, perseverance, and a willingness to learn from failure, you can develop the strength and determination to overcome obstacles and succeed in all aspects of life, feeling enlightened and knowledgeable from the lessons learned.

True growth requires a growth mindset, grit, and talent—the relentless pursuit of excellence despite obstacles, setbacks, and challenges.

A growth mindset embraces challenges as opportunities for learning, sees failures as stepping stones to success, and inspires a relentless pursuit of becoming the best version of yourself.

Developing a Growth Mindset

A growth mindset means believing your abilities and successes can improve with continued resilience, effort, and learning. An insightful resource that describes a growth mindset is the book *Mindset: The New Psychology of Success* by Carol Dweck. To develop a growth mindset, you must believe you can improve your abilities and achieve your goals through effort and learning. It is essential for facing new challenges in life, like starting a new job, moving to a new country, or even trying a new sport!

Strategies to Develop a Growth Mindset:

+ **Embrace Challenges:** Do not shy away from challenges. Instead of giving up when things get tough, view them as chances to learn and grow. Push yourself to try new things, take on new projects, and step out of your comfort zone.

+ **Focus On the Process:** Instead of fixating on the end goal, prioritize the process of learning and personal growth. Acknowledge and appreciate small achievements and keep your attention on the knowledge and skills you acquire.

+ **Learn from Failure:** When you encounter failure, do not let it make you feel inadequate. Instead, please use it to gain knowledge and enhance your skills. Analyze what went wrong, identify ways to improve, and consider how to use these insights in other aspects of your life.

+ **Cultivate a Love of Learning:** Explore novel knowledge, abilities, and adventures that captivate your attention. Adopt a passion for learning without any specific goal in mind, simply for the joy of acquiring new insights and expertise.

+ **Practice Self-Reflection:** Pausing and examining your thoughts and beliefs is essential. Be aware of when you are stuck in a fixed mindset and try to shift towards a growth mindset.

+ **Surround Yourself with Growth-Minded People**: It is beneficial to surround yourself with friends, colleagues, and mentors who have a growth mindset and encourage you to cultivate one.

A growth mindset means believing in your abilities and successes can improve with continued resilience, effort, and learning. It is essential when facing new challenges in life, like starting a new job, moving to a new country, or even trying a new sport!

A growth mindset is a belief system that shapes how you approach challenges and opportunities in life. It is based on the understanding that your abilities and intelligence can be developed through effort, persistence, and learning. When you have a growth mindset, we welcome challenges as opportunities for growth, see failures as lessons, embrace feedback, and celebrate the success of others. It empowers you to step out of your comfort zone, seek new experiences and knowledge, and achieve your goals. A growth mindset is the foundation for building a life full of resilience, creativity, and endless possibilities.

Developing a Grit Mindset

Angela Duckworth, a psychologist and researcher, is best known for her work on grit, which she defines as a combination of passion and perseverance for long-term goals. In her book *Grit: The Power of Passion and Perseverance*, Duckworth explores how grit can be developed and why it plays a crucial role in achieving success.

Grit is defined as a combination of passion and perseverance toward long-term goals. It involves maintaining effort and interest over extended periods despite facing challenges, obstacles, and setbacks. Grit is about staying committed to a pursuit, continuously working hard, and pushing through difficulties without giving up. This quality is often considered a critical factor in achieving success, as it reflects a person's ability to stay focused on their goals and persist in their efforts, even when progress is slow or difficult.

Setting clear and meaningful goals that align with your values and aspirations is essential. A strong sense of purpose and direction can provide motivation and focus to overcome obstacles and stay committed to your objectives. Adopting a positive attitude towards failure and seeing it as a natural part of the learning process can help you develop resilience and perseverance.

Feel the pride of achievement as you cultivate the habit of persevering in adversity. This involves maintaining effort and determination, even when slow progress or obstacles arise. Break your goals down into smaller, manageable tasks, and commit to taking consistent action toward achieving them. Strengthen your resilience by developing coping strategies for stress, setbacks, and failures. This may include practicing self-care, seeking support from others, and maintaining a healthy perspective on challenges. Pursue activities and goals that align with your passions and interests. When deeply passionate about something, you are more likely to stay committed and resilient in facing challenges. Get comfortable with discomfort and embrace pushing yourself outside your comfort zone. Growth often occurs when you challenge yourself and take on new experiences that stretch your abilities and capacities.

Develop self-discipline by setting clear priorities, managing time effectively, and staying focused on your goals. Practice habits such as goal setting, planning, and time management to build self-control and consistency in your actions. Be open to feedback and constructive criticism from others. Use feedback as an opportunity to learn, grow, and improve rather than as a judgment of your worth or abilities. Acknowledge and celebrate your progress, no matter how small. Recognizing your achievements and milestones can boost your motivation and reinforce your commitment to your goals. Keep a long-term perspective and remind yourself of the bigger picture. Focus on the journey of growth and development rather than getting discouraged by temporary setbacks or challenges.

Strategies to Develop Grit:

+ **Set Meaningful Goals:** Identify clear and meaningful goals that align with your values and aspirations. A strong sense of purpose and direction can provide motivation and focus to overcome obstacles, and you stay committed to your objectives.

+ **Develop a Growth Mindset:** Embrace a growth mindset, which involves viewing challenges and setbacks as opportunities for learning and growth rather than insurmountable barriers. Adopting a positive attitude towards failure and seeing it as a natural part of the learning process can help you develop resilience and perseverance.

+ **Practice Perseverance:** Cultivate the habit of persevering in adversity. This involves maintaining effort and determination even when slow progress or obstacles arise. Break your goals down into smaller, manageable tasks, and commit to taking consistent action toward achieving them.

+ **Build Resilience:** Strengthen your resilience by developing coping strategies for stress, setbacks, and failures. This may include practicing self-care, seeking support from others, and maintaining a healthy perspective on challenges.

+ **Focus on Passion:** Pursue activities and goals that align with your passions and interests. When deeply passionate about something, you are more likely to stay committed and resilient in facing challenges.

+ **Embrace Discomfort:** Accept discomfort and push yourself outside your comfort zone. Growth often occurs when you challenge yourself and take on new experiences that stretch your abilities and capabilities.

+ **Cultivate Self-Discipline:** Develop self-discipline by setting clear priorities, managing your time effectively, and staying focused on your goals. Practice habits such as goal setting, planning, and time management to build self-control and consistency in your actions.

+ **Seek Feedback:** Be open to feedback and constructive criticism from others. Use feedback as an opportunity to learn, grow, and improve rather than as a judgment of your worth or abilities.

+ **Celebrate Progress:** Take time, acknowledge, and celebrate your progress, no matter how small. Recognizing your achievements and milestones can boost your motivation and reinforce your commitment to your goals.

+ **Maintain Perspective:** Keep a long-term perspective and remind yourself of the bigger picture. Focus on the journey of growth and development rather than getting discouraged by temporary setbacks or challenges.

Developing grit involves cultivating essential qualities and habits that contribute to resilience, perseverance, and long-term success.

Grit

(gr-it) • noun

To have the determination and courage to push through any challenge or obstacle thrown your way until you succeed.

Developing a growth and grit mindset requires embracing challenges to fuel growth and meeting adversity with perseverance. It's about believing in the power of effort, adapting to setbacks, and staying committed to your goals no matter how tough the journey becomes.

Developing a Growth and Grit Mindset—Overcoming Obstacles

Developing a growth and grit mindset requires resilience and determination to navigate emotional obstacles. Often, these obstacles manifest as fear, doubt, or frustration, hindering progress and growth. However, with a growth and grit mindset, emotions are part of your journey and can be transformed into opportunities for learning and development. By acknowledging and confronting these emotions head-on, you can cultivate resilience, perseverance, and mental toughness. Rather than allowing emotions to hold you back, you can use them as fuel to propel yourself forward, overcoming obstacles and achieving your goals.

Strategies to Overcome Challenging Obstacles:

+ **Identify and Acknowledge Your Emotions:** Start by identifying and acknowledging your emotions to overcome obstacles. Allow yourself to feel complex emotions without judgment and recognize that it is okay to experience them.

+ **Practice Self-Care:** Prioritizing physical and emotional well-being enhances resilience and helps manage challenging emotions. Ensure you obtain adequate sleep, maintain a regular exercise routine, follow a nutritious diet, and incorporate relaxation methods like meditation or deep breathing into your daily routine.

+ **Seek Support:** If you are struggling with your emotions, seek support from trusted friends, family members, or consider working with a therapist or counselor. Talking to someone can help you process your feelings and find effective coping strategies.

+ **Practice Mindfulness:** Mindfulness means being present in the moment without any judgment. It allows you to observe your thoughts and emotions without being overwhelmed.

+ **Challenge Negative Thoughts:** It is common to face emotional obstacles that trigger negative self-talk and limiting beliefs. To overcome them, try questioning the validity of these thoughts and seeking evidence that proves them wrong.

+ **Take Small Steps:** It is essential to make changes to overcome emotional obstacles with small, achievable goals and take gradual steps toward reaching them. Remember, overcoming emotional obstacles takes time and effort, and asking for help is okay. Be patient with yourself, and celebrate your progress, no matter how small.

Overcoming obstacles in developing a growth and grit mindset involves recognizing challenges as opportunities for growth rather than barriers to success. It requires resilience in the face of setbacks and a willingness to persist in pursuing long-term goals. By embracing failure as a natural part of the learning process and reframing setbacks as valuable learning experiences, you can cultivate the perseverance needed to overcome adversity. Moreover, seeking support from mentors, coaches, and peers can provide helpful guidance and encouragement along the journey. By adopting a growth-oriented mindset and fostering grit, you can confidently navigate challenges and emerge stronger and more resilient.

Dawn Staley embodies resilience and determination.
Her journey, marked by overcoming obstacles and breaking
barriers, inspires others to lead with courage, pursue
their passions, and never back down from a challenge.

Dawn Staley's Story—Grit and Growth Mindset

Dawn Staley's story is one of resilience, determination, and triumph against the odds. Born in a tough neighborhood in Philadelphia, she faced numerous challenges growing up, including poverty and the lure of street life. However, basketball became her refuge—a way to channel her energy and ambition into something positive.

Despite her small stature, Dawn's talent and work ethic propelled her to become one of the most dominant players in women's basketball history. She led her teams to multiple championships, earning accolades and recognition at collegiate and professional levels. Along the way, she faced skepticism and discrimination due to her race and gender, but she refused to let it deter her.

Off the court, Dawn has been equally impressive. She has become a respected coach, leading her teams to success while mentoring young athletes and advocating for social justice causes. Her leadership and tenacity have earned her the admiration of fans and peers, cementing her legacy as a true trailblazer in women's sports.

Through it all, Dawn Staley's story is a powerful reminder that anything is possible with grit, determination, and a relentless pursuit of excellence. She is a shining example of how resilience and perseverance can turn adversity into opportunity and inspire others to reach for their dreams, no matter what the obstacles.

Process Over Product—Growth and Grit Mindset

Developing a mindset that prioritizes process over product involves shifting your focus from solely focusing on outcomes or results to valuing the journey, growth, and learning that occurs along the way.

Critical Steps to Develop a Process-Oriented Mindset:

1. **Set Process-Oriented Goals:** Instead of solely focusing on the result, set goals that emphasize the actions, efforts, and habits required to achieve success. Define specific processes or steps that will contribute to your progress and development.

2. **Embrace Learning and Growth:** Approach tasks and challenges with a mindset of continuous learning and growth. See each experience as an opportunity to acquire new skills, deepen your knowledge, and develop professionally and personally. Embrace the idea that mistakes and setbacks are valuable learning opportunities.

3. **Prioritize Skill Development:** Focus on developing your skills and capabilities rather than solely pursuing achievements. Invest time and effort honing your abilities, seeking feedback, and engaging in deliberate practice. Emphasize your progress in acquiring and refining skills, regardless of immediate outcomes.

4. **Cultivate Present-Moment Awareness:** Practice mindfulness and be fully present in your tasks. Shift your attention from future results to the current moment, immersing yourself in the process entirely. Embrace the joy and fulfillment from being engaged and absorbed in your work.

5. **Reflect on the Process:** Regularly reflect on your experiences and the processes you engage in. Consider what practical strategies, approaches,

or techniques align with your goals. Reflect on refining and improving your processes and adjust based on lessons learned.

6. **Value Iteration and Feedback:** Embrace a mindset of iteration and improvement. See feedback from yourself or others as valuable input for enhancing your processes. Embrace a willingness to adapt, make changes, and iterate based on new insights and information.

7. **Celebrate Milestones and Progress:** Acknowledge and celebrate your progress, regardless of the outcome. Recognize the effort, dedication, and growth that occurs during the process. Reward yourself for milestones reached and milestones exceeded.

8. **Cultivate Patience and Resilience:** Understand that meaningful growth and development take time. Cultivate patience and resilience, recognizing that progress may not always be linear. Stay committed to the process, even in the face of challenges or setbacks, knowing each step contributes to your overall growth.

Adopting a process-oriented mindset shifts your attention from external outcomes to internal growth and development. By embracing the journey, valuing the process, and finding fulfillment in the present moment, you can experience profound satisfaction and personal fulfillment in your endeavors.

Success is not just about reaching the destination; it is about embracing the journey, focusing on the process, and finding joy in pursuing excellence.

My Story on Writing This Book—Growth and Grit Mindset

Writing this book has been a journey of exploration, creativity, and discipline. It started with an idea or inspiration, then developed into a concept, theme, or outline guiding my writing. I conducted research, brainstormed, and planned, which helped shape the narrative and structure. As I wrote, the story evolved and unfolded through drafting, revising, and refining, often requiring multiple edits to sharpen the language, clarify ideas, and ensure coherence.

The most significant challenge for me was the resistance. In his book *The War of Art*, Steve Pressfield describes resistance as the main antagonist in any creative or personal endeavor. It manifests fear, self-sabotage, procrastination, and doubt. Pressfield argues that it's a universal force everyone must confront. Resistance comes in many forms, including fear, procrastination, self-doubt, and distractions, and it affects anyone trying to create, change, or pursue their true calling.

Battling the resistance is an ongoing struggle. The negative feedback loop of thoughts is a continuous battle. By consistently doing the work and adopting a professional mindset, I developed habits and strategies to fight the resistance and overcome the barriers that hold me back. By committing to a regular practice, we can push through resistance and build momentum toward our goals.

Lessons Learned:

- Set a time to write every day.
- Set a place where I am not distracted or interrupted.
- Write without judging—edit at a later time.
- Emphasize the writing process.
- When stuck, get away from the work or project.
- Set daily, weekly, and monthly goals.
- Get help when needed.
- Celebrate small wins.

Developing a growth and grit mindset means embracing challenges as opportunities, staying resilient through setbacks, and continuously striving to improve.
It's about believing in the power of effort and persistence to achieve your goals.

Summary

The growth and grit mindsets are potent frameworks that drive our personal and professional success. A growth mindset is based on the belief that abilities and intelligence can be developed through effort and practice. It encourages you to embrace challenges, learn from failures, and continuously seek improvement. On the other hand, a grit mindset involves perseverance, passion, and long-term growth. The growth and grit mindsets are highly effective frameworks that propel you toward personal and professional triumphs. A growth mindset is rooted in the idea that abilities and intelligence can be honed through exertion and repetition. It motivates you to confront challenges, learn from failures, and strive for progress. In contrast, a grit mindset entails persistence, enthusiasm, and unwavering dedication toward attaining objectives. It underscores resilience and the capacity to surmount setbacks and hurdles.

Both mindsets work together to enhance your personal growth and professional success. When we adopt a growth mindset, we become receptive to new opportunities, perceive challenges as chances to learn and grow, and strive for continuous self-improvement. Conversely, a grit mindset instills the tenacity and resilience required to remain steadfast in pursuing long-term objectives and surmounting any obstacles.

Action Plan

Develop a Growth and Grit Mindset with the Following Steps:

1. Develop a journal titled 'Growth and Grit Mindsets'.

2. Review the definitions of both growth and grit mindsets.

3. Write down what goals and successes that you would like to achieve.

4. Write down obstacles that may get in the way of developing these mindsets.

5. Write down strategies to overcome obstacles that may get in your way.

6. Review periodically and adjust strategies that can help you achieve success and your desired goals.

CHAPTER 7

Developing Mental Strength

"You have power over your mind, not outside events. Realize this, and you will find strength."

Marcus Aurelius—*Meditations*

Mental Strength—Definition

Mental strength is coping effectively with challenges, setbacks, and stress while maintaining a positive outlook and control over one's thoughts, emotions, and behaviors. It involves resilience, perseverance, and the capacity to adapt to adversity without being overwhelmed.

Mental strength involves a combination of cognitive, emotional, and behavioral skills that enable you to thrive in adversity and challenges, leading to greater resilience, well-being, and success.

Mental Strength Characteristics:

+ **Resilience:** Bouncing back from setbacks, failures, and difficult circumstances, learning and growing from your experiences rather than being defeated by them.

- ✦ **Emotional Regulation:** Managing emotions effectively, staying calm and composed in stressful situations, and not allowing negative emotions to dictate your actions.
- ✦ **Positive Thinking:** Maintaining a positive mindset, focusing on solutions rather than dwelling on problems, and looking for opportunities for growth and improvement.
- ✦ **Determination:** Developing a strong sense of purpose and commitment, staying focused on your goals, and facing obstacles or setbacks.
- ✦ **Self-discipline:** Controlling impulses, maintaining healthy habits, and staying on track even when faced with distractions or temptations.
- ✦ **Adaptability:** Being flexible, open-minded, and able to adjust your approach and strategies in response to changing circumstances or the latest information.

Mental strength involves a combination of cognitive, emotional, and behavioral skills that enable you to thrive in adversity and challenges, leading to greater resilience, well-being, and success.

Developing personal strengths and skills is an ongoing journey of self-discovery and intentional effort. It requires recognizing what empowers you, embracing challenges that stretch your abilities, and consistently refining your craft to unlock your full potential.

Developing Mental Strength Skills

Developing mental strength involves integrating cognitive, emotional, and behavioral skills. It requires cultivating a resilient mindset capable of navigating life's challenges with grit and adaptability. Cognitive skills include the ability to focus, think critically, and problem-solve effectively, enabling you to approach obstacles with clarity and determination. Emotionally, mental strength involves mastering self-awareness, emotional regulation, and optimism, empowering us to manage stress, setbacks, and uncertainties with composure and positivity. Additionally, behavioral skills entail adopting proactive habits, such as goal setting, time management, and assertive communication, to translate thoughts and emotions into constructive actions. By honing these interconnected abilities, you can enhance your capacity to thrive amidst adversity, achieve personal and professional goals, and foster overall well-being. Ultimately, developing mental strength is a continuous journey of self-discovery and growth characterized by resilience, courage, and inner strength.

Steps to Help You Strengthen Your Mental Resilience:

+ **Identify Areas for Improvement**: Reflect on your current strengths and weaknesses regarding mental resilience. Identify areas where you would like to develop greater strength, such as managing stress, handling setbacks, or maintaining a positive mindset.

+ **Set Clear Goals**: Establish clear and achievable goals for building mental strength. Break down larger goals into smaller, actionable steps to make progress more manageable and measurable.

+ **Practice Resilience-Building Exercises**: Engage in activities that challenge you to overcome obstacles and setbacks. This could include setting small challenges for yourself, facing your fears, or learning from past failures to grow stronger.

+ **Cultivate Positive Thinking**: Train your mind to focus on solutions rather than dwelling on problems. Practice gratitude, positive self-talk, and reframing negative thoughts into more empowering perspectives.

+ **Develop Emotional Regulation Skills:** Learn techniques for managing your emotions effectively, such as deep breathing, mindfulness meditation, or journaling. Practice staying calm and composed in stressful situations to avoid reacting impulsively.

+ **Build Determination and Persistence:** Cultivate a strong sense of purpose and commitment to your goals. Stay focused on what you can control and persevere when facing obstacles or setbacks. Celebrate small victories along the way to stay motivated.

+ **Practice Self-Discipline:** Develop healthy habits and routines that support your mental and emotional well-being. This could include regular exercise, adequate sleep, healthy eating, and time management strategies to stay organized and focused.

+ **Seek Support and Guidance:** If you are struggling, do not hesitate to contact friends, family, or professional support. Surround yourself with positive influences and mentors who can provide encouragement, advice, and perspective.

+ **Learn from Setbacks and Challenges:** Embrace failures and setbacks as opportunities for growth and learning. Reflect on what went wrong, identify lessons learned, and adjust your approach to become more resilient.

+ **Stay Flexible and Adaptable:** Practice being flexible and open-minded in approaching life's challenges. Be willing to adjust your strategies and perspectives as needed in response to changing circumstances or new information.

By consistently practicing these steps and incorporating resilience-building habits into your daily life, you can strengthen your mental resilience and thrive in adversity and challenges.

Mindfulness meditation is a powerful tool for developing mental strength. It trains the mind to stay present, cultivating awareness and resilience in the face of stress. We build the foundation for clarity, focus, and emotional fortitude by quieting distractions and embracing inner peace.

Mindfulness and Meditation—Mental Strength Tools

In his book *The Mindful Athlete*, George Mumford discusses, *"Mindfulness is the awareness that arises from paying attention, on purpose, in the present moment and non-judgmentally."*

George Mumford is a well-known mindfulness coach and author, famous for his work with elite athletes such as Michael Jordan, Kobe Bryant, and other members of the Chicago Bulls and Los Angeles Lakers during their championship runs in the 1990s and early 2000s.

Mindfulness is intentionally paying attention to the present moment without judgment. It involves fully understanding our thoughts, feelings, bodily sensations, and environment. Mindfulness emphasizes acceptance and non-reactivity to whatever is happening, allowing you to cultivate a greater sense of clarity, calmness, and inner peace. You can develop greater self-awareness, emotional regulation, and overall well-being through mindfulness practices such as meditation, breathing exercises, and mindful movement.

Meditation is a technique for training the mind to attain a state of mental clarity, relaxation, and heightened awareness. It involves focusing on and engaging in specific exercises promoting deep concentration, mindfulness, or contemplation.

During meditation, you typically aim to cultivate a calm and peaceful mental state by directing your attention to a specific object, such as the breath, a mantra, a visual image, or bodily sensations. The intention is to observe and acknowledge thoughts, emotions, and sensations without judgment or attachment, allowing them to come and go while maintaining a present-moment awareness.

Meditation practices vary across distinct cultures and traditions, each with their unique approach. Examples include mindfulness meditation, transcendental meditation, and loving-kindness meditation. These practices may involve sitting or lying comfortably, following specific breathing patterns, repeating mantras or affirmations, visualizing images, or participating in guided meditation sessions.

**When the mind is allowed to relax,
inspiration often follows.**

Primary Goals of Meditation and Mindfulness

+   **Cultivating Mindfulness:** Developing a heightened awareness and being fully present in the current moment.

+   **Relaxation and Stress Reduction:** These practices promote relaxation, reduce physiological and psychological stress responses, and foster a sense of calm and tranquility.

+   **Emotional Well-Being:** Enhancing emotional regulation, increasing self-awareness, and fostering a sense of inner peace and happiness.

+   **Mental Focus and Clarity:** Improving concentration, enhancing cognitive abilities, and fostering mental clarity and alertness.

+   **Self-Exploration and Personal Growth:** Facilitating self-reflection, exploring thoughts, beliefs, and emotions, and promoting personal growth and self-discovery.

In summary, meditation and mindfulness offer numerous benefits for both mental and physical well-being. Practicing mindfulness helps you stay present and fully engaged in the moment, reducing stress and promoting emotional balance. Regular meditation can improve focus, enhance self-awareness, and foster a greater sense of calm, leading to better decision-making and overall mental clarity. Additionally, mindfulness and meditation have been shown to lower blood pressure, improve sleep, and boost immune function. Cultivating a more centered and resilient mind enables you to manage life's challenges better, increase your happiness, and achieve a more profound sense of inner peace.

"As much as we pump iron and we run to build our strength up, we need to build our mental strength up . . . so we can focus . . . so we can be in concert with one another."

Phil Jackson—World Championship Basketball Coach—
Eleven Rings: The Soul of Success

Meditation Research

The science of meditation is a growing field of study that explores the effects of various meditation practices on the mind, body, and overall well-being. Over the past few decades, scientific research has increasingly focused on understanding the mechanisms underlying the benefits of meditation and its potential impact on mental and physical health. Studies have shown that regular meditation practice can have a range of positive effects on the brain and body.

The science of meditation has been explored and studied by researchers and scientists from various fields, including psychology, neuroscience, medicine, and contemplative studies.

Key Findings from Scientific Research on Meditation:

+ **Neuroplasticity:** Research has shown that meditation can enhance neuroplasticity, which refers to the brain's capacity to adapt and restructure. The practice has been linked to modifications in the structure and function of brain regions responsible for attention, emotional regulation, and self-awareness.

+ **Cognitive Benefits:** Regular meditation has been associated with enhanced attention, working memory, cognitive flexibility, and problem-solving skills. Additionally, it has the potential to boost creativity and decision-making abilities.

+ **Emotional Well-Being:** Meditation has displayed encouraging outcomes in alleviating stress, anxiety, and depression symptoms. It can aid in managing emotions, improving stress endurance, and fostering inner tranquility and overall wellness.

+ **Physical Health:** Research shows meditation can positively impact physical health. It has been linked to lower blood pressure, enhanced immune function, and reduced inflammation. Additionally, meditation may aid in managing pain and improving sleep quality.

+ **Brainwave Patterns:** Various types of meditation are linked to distinct brainwave patterns. Mindfulness meditation, for instance, can elevate alpha and theta brainwaves associated with relaxation and a focused, peaceful state of mind.

+ **Mind-Body Connection:** Meditation practices strongly emphasize the connection between the mind and body. Research has indicated that meditation increases body awareness, reduces somatic symptoms, and improves mind-body integration.

+ **Psychological Well-Being:** Meditation has been linked to various benefits, such as heightened self-awareness, self-compassion, and better psychological health. It can increase positive emotions, promote empathy and compassion, and enhance interpersonal connections.

Our understanding of meditation from a scientific perspective is still developing, and further research is necessary. It is important to note that each meditation technique can have unique effects, and everyone's experience may differ. Through scientific research, the exploration of meditation has revealed its potential benefits on one's mental, emotional, and physical well-being. Research has shown that integrating a consistent meditation routine into daily life can positively impact different areas.

"Meditation is not evasion; it is a serene encounter with reality."

Thich Nhat Hanh, Vietnamese Zen Buddhist monk

Meditation and Mindfulness Benefits

Regular meditation and mindfulness practices can have benefits, including significantly improving physical, mental, and emotional well-being.

Essential Advantages of Meditation and Mindfulness:

+ **Stress Reduction:** You can use meditation to manage and reduce stress. This practice can trigger the body's relaxation response, leading to a decrease in stress hormones and a sense of calmness and tranquility.

+ **Improved Mental Clarity and Focus:** Regular meditation can boost concentration and attention span. It aids in conditioning the mind to remain fixated on the current moment, lessening mental disturbances and amplifying clarity of thought.

+ **Emotional Well-Being:** Meditation can develop emotional resilience and stability by regulating emotions. It can diminish negative emotions like anxiety and depression while encouraging positive ones like happiness, contentment, and compassion.

+ **Increased Self-Awareness:** Meditation cultivates self-awareness by prompting you to observe your thoughts, emotions, and physical sensations without critical evaluation. This increased self-awareness facilitates a better understanding of yourself and your behavioral patterns and enables you to respond consciously instead of impulsively.

+ **Enhanced Cognitive Abilities:** Studies show meditation positively affects cognitive abilities like memory, problem-solving, and decision-making. It also encourages neuroplasticity, the brain's capacity to adjust and transform, and may enhance mental performance.

+ **Better Sleep:** Incorporating regular meditation into your routines can improve sleep quality and decrease insomnia symptoms. Meditation can help achieve a more tranquil and rejuvenating sleep experience by inducing relaxation and calming racing thoughts.

+ **Physical Health Benefits:** Meditation provides physical health benefits, including reducing blood pressure, enhancing the immune system, decreasing inflammation, and promoting better cardiovascular health. Moreover, it can encourage healthier habits and lifestyle choices, like practicing mindful eating and engaging in more physical activity.

+ **Increased Resilience and Stress Coping Skills:** Through mindfulness training, meditation cultivates the ability to be more present and less reactive to stress, which fosters resilience and equips you with effective coping strategies. It strengthens your capacity to navigate challenges and recover from adversity.

+ **Improved Relationships:** By practicing meditation, you can develop valuable qualities such as empathy, compassion, and non-judgment.

These qualities can contribute to more fulfilling and harmonious relationships with others. Additionally, meditation can enhance communication, understanding, and emotional connection between us.

+ **Spiritual Growth and Self-Transcendence:** If you are looking for ways to enhance your spiritual growth or experience a stronger sense of connection, practicing meditation can be an effective means of achieving self-transcendence, self-discovery, and a more profound comprehension of the interconnectedness of all living things.

It is important to note that the benefits of meditation and mindfulness may vary from person to person, and consistent practice is necessary to experience these benefits. To find the meditation technique that suits you best, you should experiment with various styles. Trying different ones would be helpful.

> "I've seen firsthand the transformative power of mindfulness through the MBSR program. It's not just about managing stress; it's about reclaiming control over your life and finding peace in the present moment."
>
> Michael Baime, M.D.—UPENN—Penn Program for Mindfulness

MBSR—Mindfulness-Based Stress Reduction— The Definition of Mindfulness

"Mindfulness is the awareness that arises through paying attention, on purpose, in the present moment, non-judgmentally," says Jon Kabat-Zinn. "And then I sometimes add, in the service of self-understanding and wisdom."

Mindfulness-Based Stress Reduction (MBSR) is a program established and proven through evidence. It combines mindfulness meditation, yoga, and mind-body awareness techniques to help you manage stress, reduce anxiety, and improve overall well-being. Dr. Jon Kabat-Zinn developed MBSR at the University of Massachusetts Medical Center in the late 1970s.

The program usually consists of an eight-week course that involves weekly group sessions, daily mindfulness practices at home, and guided meditations. Participants learn mindfulness practices like body scan meditation, mindful breathing, and yoga stretches. These practices aim to increase mindfulness, cultivate non-judgmental acceptance, and foster inner peace and clarity.

The purpose of MBSR is to aid people in cultivating mindfulness through nonjudgmental awareness in the present moment. This program empowers you with practical techniques to handle stress, overcome obstacles, and enhance your overall wellness. MBSR is typically conducted in a group format spanning eight weeks, with each session running for approximately two and a half hours per week.

Participants learn mindfulness practices like body scan meditation, mindful breathing, and yoga stretches. It is important to note that MBSR should not be seen as a substitute for medical or psychological treatment. Rather than being a standalone solution, it is a complementary approach that can support overall well-being and help reduce stress. Before starting MBSR, individuals with specific medical or mental health conditions should consult healthcare professionals.

Vital Elements of Mindfulness-Based Stress Reduction Include:

1. **Mindfulness Meditation:** During the program, you are instructed in various mindfulness meditation techniques, including breath-focused meditation, body scan meditation, and mindful movement activities such as yoga or walking meditation. These practices foster the capacity to be fully present in the current moment and to cultivate a non-critical awareness of one's thoughts, feelings, and physical sensations.

2. **Body Awareness:** MBSR focuses on enhancing awareness of bodily sensations and the connection between the mind and body. Participants are taught to observe and investigate bodily sensations and tensions to comprehend and cope with stress responses.

3. **Stress Reduction Techniques:** MBSR provides various techniques and coping strategies to reduce stress that can be incorporated into daily life. These techniques involve being mindful in everyday tasks, responding instead of reacting to stressors, and cultivating a non-judgmental perspective towards oneself and others.

4. **Group Support:** The MBSR program is usually conducted in a group to encourage participants to exchange experiences, learn from one another, and get support in their mindfulness practice. Group discussions and reflections provide a sense of community and help enhance knowledge.

Extensive research has proven the effectiveness of MBSR in reducing stress levels, enhancing emotional well-being, promoting focus and attention, and building resilience. This technique is widely utilized in various environments such as healthcare, workplaces, and community programs.

The Primary Goals of MBSR:

1. **Reduce Stress:** MBSR aims to help you recognize and respond to stress more adaptively. Participants can prevent stress from escalating and manage its effects more effectively by learning to be present and non-reactive to stressors.

2. **Enhance Resilience:** Through regular mindfulness practices, participants can develop emotional resilience and coping skills to navigate challenging situations with greater stability and inner strength.

3. **Improve Mental Health:** MBSR is an effective intervention for reducing symptoms of anxiety, depression, and other psychological disorders. You can better regulate your emotions and maintain psychological well-being by cultivating mindfulness.

4. **Increase Self-Awareness:** Mindfulness practices encourage self-reflection and greater self-awareness. Participants become more attuned to

their thoughts, emotions, and physical sensations, which can lead to enhanced self-understanding and personal growth.

5. **Enhance Focus and Concentration:** Regular mindfulness practice has improved attention and concentration, helping individuals stay focused and present in their daily activities.

It is worth mentioning that although MBSR is frequently taught in a structured program, anyone can practice and apply the principles and techniques of mindfulness in their daily life, even without formal training.

George Mumford's mindfulness and mental training have transformed athletes and teams. His teachings emphasize being present, self-awareness, and inner calm, showing that mental strength is essential for sustained success, just as much as physical skill.

George Mumford—*The Mindful Athlete*

In 1993, when Michael Jordan left the Chicago Bulls to play baseball, the team faced a crisis. Coach Phil Jackson, a mindfulness practitioner, sought help from Dr. Jon Kabat-Zinn to teach mindfulness techniques to the struggling team. Jon Kabat-Zinn introduced Jackson to Mumford, and their partnership began.

George Mumford's book *The Mindful Athlete* emphasizes mindfulness and its practical application in daily life, sports, and performance. George Mumford is a renowned mindfulness teacher who has assisted sports teams, athletes, and organizations in integrating mindfulness practices for improved well-being and performance. Mumford has since worked with Jackson, his championship-winning teams, corporate executives, Olympians, and athletes in various sports.

Key Insights George Mumford Emphasizes:

+ **Mindfulness as Presence:** Mumford advises us to cultivate a mentality of living in the present, redirecting our focus toward the current moment. Consistently practicing this approach can improve performance by decreasing distractions and enhancing concentration and attentiveness.

+ **Non-Judgmental Awareness:** Mumford emphasizes the importance of observing one's thoughts, emotions, and sensations without passing judgment. Developing a non-judgmental mindset can help us manage stress, overcome obstacles, and respond effectively to different situations.

+ **Acceptance and Letting Go:** Mumford's teachings emphasize embracing the present moment and relinquishing attachment to past experiences and outcomes. This practice can foster inner peace, reduce performance anxiety, and enhance adaptability in the face of change. By letting go of expectations, we can concentrate on the present and discover greater contentment.

+ **Emotional Regulation:** Mumford believes being mindful is crucial in managing emotions. By becoming more aware of our emotions and choosing not to react impulsively, we can effectively deal with them and make wiser choices, thus enhancing our emotional well-being.

+ **Visualization and Mental Imagery:** Mumford employs visualization and mental imagery methods to aid athletes and performers in enhancing their focus, confidence, and overall performance. This entails fostering positive mental states by envisioning success and improving one's ability to implement skills and strategies successfully; proper execution is essential.

Overall, George Mumford's teachings revolve around utilizing mindfulness to cultivate presence, enhance performance, manage emotions, and find greater well-being. While his work is often associated with sports, the principles and techniques he teaches can be applied in various domains of life to support personal growth, resilience, and overall mental and emotional well-being.

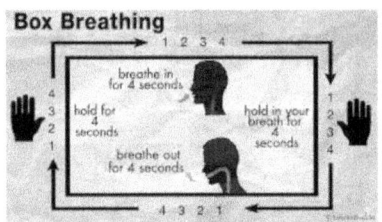

Box breathing is a simple yet powerful practice that helps clear the mind and restore focus. By controlling my breath, I calm my nervous system and build resilience in the face of stress, empowering me to stay centered and present, no matter the challenge.

Box Breathing

Box breathing, also known as square breathing, is a mental strength technique. It involves inhaling, holding the breath, exhaling, and then holding again, each for a count of four. This method calms the mind, reduces stress, and improves focus. Box breathing helps to activate the parasympathetic nervous system, promoting relaxation and mental clarity.

Athletes, military personnel, and individuals in high-stress situations commonly use this technique to build resilience, enhance concentration, and maintain emotional control. As a mental strength exercise, it trains the mind to stay present and manage anxiety, making it a powerful tool for developing mental toughness.

Box Breathing Steps:

1. Find a comfortable seated position and relax your body.

2. Inhale slowly and deeply through your nose to a count of four. Imagine drawing a line on the side of the square.

3. Hold your breath for a count of four at the top of your inhalation. Imagine moving along the top of the square.

4. Exhale wholly and slowly through your mouth to a count of four, releasing tension and stress. Imagine moving down the side of the square.

5. At the bottom of your exhalation, hold your breath for a count of four. Imagine moving along the bottom of the square.

6. Repeat the inhaling, holding, exhaling, and holding cycle for several rounds or as long as desired.

To master box breathing, you must concentrate on your breath and maintain a steady count for every stage of the breathing process. As you practice this method, you may find it helpful to imagine drawing a square with your breath.

If you are feeling stressed or anxious, box breathing can be a valuable technique for helping you feel more relaxed and focused. This simple practice can be done anywhere, anytime, and has been shown to regulate the autonomic nervous system. Give it a try next time you need to refresh your mind and regain focus.

Journaling is a tool of reflection and growth. By putting my thoughts onto paper, I clarify my intentions, confront challenges, and chart a path forward. It's more than a practice—it's a personal mirror that helps me understand my emotions, track my progress, and continuously evolve.

Journaling—Mental Strength Technique

Journaling is a powerful mental strength technique. It involves regularly writing down thoughts, feelings, goals, and experiences, which helps build self-awareness, emotional resilience, and clarity. By reflecting on challenges, identifying patterns, and processing emotions, journaling allows you to understand your inner world better and develop coping strategies.

Additionally, journaling promotes problem-solving and helps reframe negative thoughts into constructive ones. Over time, this practice can strengthen mental resilience, helping you manage stress, track progress, and maintain a positive mindset. As a result, journaling is a powerful tool for developing mental strength and fostering personal growth.

Journaling, which involves recording your thoughts, feelings, and experiences in a journal, is an excellent practice for personal growth, self-reflection, and maintaining good health.

Journaling Benefits:

+ **Emotional Release and Processing:** Journaling provides a secure outlet for expressing and letting go of emotions. It enables you to delve into and deal with intricate feelings, frustrations, and challenges, thereby promoting better emotional wellness and a sense of relief.

+ **Self-Reflection and Self-Awareness:** Keeping a journal regularly can enhance self-reflection and self-awareness. You can better comprehend your behavior, values, and beliefs by expressing your experiences, thoughts, and patterns through writing. Journaling aids in recognizing recurring themes, strengths, and areas for improvement and defining personal goals and aspirations.

- **Stress Reduction:** Writing in a journal can provide emotional and mental relief from stress. When you jot down your worries and concerns, they can alleviate the burden of these thoughts. Furthermore, journaling can help you reframe stressful situations, gain new perspectives, and develop effective coping strategies.

- **Enhanced Creativity and Problem-Solving:** Keeping a journal can enhance creativity and improve problem-solving abilities. By freely writing or brainstorming in a journal, you can stimulate the flow of ideas and insights, leading to fresh perspectives, exploring possibilities, and developing innovative solutions to overcome challenges.

- **Improved Clarity and Focus:** Journaling can enhance clarity of thought and concentration. It enables you to structure your ideas, express your thoughts, and develop a more profound comprehension of complicated topics. Journaling can aid in unscrambling disordered thoughts, prioritizing tasks, and making clearer decisions.

- **Personal Growth and Self-Development:** Journaling is highly beneficial for personal growth and self-development as it helps record progress, achievements, and lessons learned. It allows you to monitor your goals, assess your actions, and pinpoint improvement areas. Consistent journaling cultivates a growth mindset and a dedication to self-improvement.

- **Emotional Healing and Trauma Recovery:** Writing in a journal can be a valuable therapeutic aid in emotional healing and recovery from traumatic experiences. It offers a secure channel to work through and let go of challenging emotions associated with past events. Doing so can assist in comprehending traumatic incidents, discovering significance, and promoting recovery and endurance.

+ **Improved Communication Skills:** Keeping a journal can improve communication skills by allowing you to express your thoughts and emotions effectively. This enhanced self-expression can translate into better communication with others in different areas of your life.

+ **Record of Memories and Life Events:** Journaling is a great way to record personal memories, experiences, and life events. It allows you to document important moments, achievements, and reflections. Reviewing past journal entries can inspire feelings of thankfulness, reminiscence, and acknowledgment of personal development.

+ **Stress Management and Sleep Quality:** Writing a reflective journal before going to sleep can be beneficial in unloading the mind, reducing overthinking, and improving sleep quality. This practice lets you process the day's events, recognize accomplishments, and release your worries before resting.

Remember, there is no right or wrong way to journal; you can tailor your approach to suit your needs and preferences. Whether through stream-of-consciousness writing, gratitude journaling, goal-setting, or specific prompts, journaling can be a valuable tool for personal exploration, self-expression, and overall well-being.

My Story—Developing Mental Strength

In 2010, I worked in a toxic environment. The COO of the company I worked for bullied many of his employees, including me. He frequently made sarcastic and derogatory comments, which left me feeling overwhelmed and out of control. I was constantly stressed, and my thinking was scattered. I felt stuck and frustrated.

Thankfully, a friend suggested I enroll in a mindfulness meditation class called MBSR. As I mentioned previously, MBSR stands for Mindfulness-Based Stress Reduction and is based on a program developed by Jon Kabat-Zinn. Jon Kabat-Zinn is associated with the Center for

Mindfulness in Medicine, Health Care, and Society at the University of Massachusetts Medical School.

Developing mindfulness meditation became crucial for regaining clarity and calm. I began by integrating simple mindfulness practices into my daily routine, such as focused breathing exercises and brief moments of reflection. Initially, it was tough to quiet my racing mind, but I committed to setting aside a few minutes each day to sit quietly and observe my thoughts without judgment.

As I continued practicing, I noticed a gradual shift. I was able to detach from the stress and gain a clearer perspective on my problems. This new-found awareness helped me recognize the difference between immediate stress and long-term solutions, allowing me to approach challenges with greater composure and insight. Over time, mindfulness became a reliable anchor, helping me navigate periods of intense stress and regain control over my thoughts and emotions.

Mental strength is the foundation of resilience and perseverance. It's about staying focused under pressure, embracing challenges, and pushing through obstacles to grow stronger with every experience.

Summary

Meditation, mindfulness, and journaling are steadfast allies in pursuing mental strength. We forge resilience, cultivate clarity, and nurture self-awareness through these disciplines.

You can cultivate a more profound connection with yourself and others through mindfulness, meditation, and journaling, leading to greater empathy, compassion, and overall life satisfaction. Practicing mindfulness enables people to live in the present moment, free from the distractions of the past and future, and to develop a non-judgmental and compassionate attitude towards their experiences. Moreover, mindfulness practices promote emotional regulation, improved focus and concentration, and enhanced self-awareness, helping you manage stress, anxiety, and other mental health challenges effectively. Mindfulness, meditation, and journaling provide valuable tools for navigating life's challenges with greater ease, resilience, and inner peace.

Action Steps

By following this action plan, you can gradually develop a sustainable meditation and mindfulness practice that enhances your well-being and helps you navigate life's challenges with greater ease and clarity.

Action Plan to Develop Meditation, Mindfulness, and Journaling:

1. **Take a Course on Mindfulness and Meditation**
   + Look for meditation courses online or in person.
   + Research qualified programs and instructors.
   + Research MBSR courses in your local community.

2. **Set Clear Goals**
   + Define your purpose: Why do you want to practice meditation and mindfulness?
   + Set achievable goals, such as reducing stress or improving focus.

3. **Create a Dedicated Space**
   + Find a quiet, comfortable space for meditation.
   + Use calming décor to make the space inviting.

4. **Start with Short Sessions**
   + Begin with five to ten-minute sessions and aim for consistency.
   + Learn basic techniques
   + Focus on your breath and body scan techniques.
   + Use guided meditation resources if needed.

5. **Incorporate Mindfulness into Daily Activities**
    + Practice being present in everyday tasks.

6. **Join a Meditation Community**
    + Consider joining a meditation group or class for support.

7. **Track Your Progress**
    + Keep a meditation journal to record your experiences and reflections.

8. **Be Patient and Compassionate**
    + Understand that progress takes time and effort.
    + Be kind to yourself during the practice.

9. **Write Down in a Journal**
    + Thoughts and thinking
    + Successes
    + Obstacles
    + Daily, weekly, and long-term goals

CHAPTER 8

Overcoming Procrastination—Tools and Techniques

"If you want to stop procrastinating, you don't need more self-discipline, but a more effective way to manage your time."

Francesco Cirillo—Author—*The Pomodoro Technique*

Procrastination—Definition

Procrastination is delaying or postponing tasks or actions that need to be accomplished, often despite knowing that doing so may have negative consequences. It involves voluntarily putting off tasks, assignments, or responsibilities, typically favoring less critical or more enjoyable activities. Procrastination can lead to increased stress, missed deadlines, decreased productivity, and guilt or regret. It is an expected behavior that we struggle with to varying degrees and can affect personal and professional aspects of life.

Key Characteristics of Procrastination Include:

+ **Intentional Delay**: Procrastination is a voluntary delay in getting started or completing tasks. It is not typically the result of external factors preventing you from working on a task.

- **Choosing Distractions**: Procrastinators often engage in distracting activities, such as watching TV, checking social media, or cleaning, instead of working on tasks.

- **Negative Consequences**: Procrastination can lead to negative consequences, such as missed deadlines, increased stress, reduced productivity, and lower-quality work.

- **Lack of Time Management**: Procrastinators need help with time management and may underestimate the time required to complete tasks.

- **Mood-Related**: Procrastination can be related to emotions and mood. People may need to work on tasks that make them anxious, bored, or overwhelmed.

- **Irrational Delay**: Procrastination often involves unreasonable delay, where individuals delay tasks even when it is not in their best interest.

Procrastination cycles can feel like a never-ending loop, but breaking them begins with awareness. Recognizing the pattern allows us to take small, deliberate actions that disrupt the cycle, turning delay into progress and transforming hesitation into momentum.

Procrastination Cycles

Barbara Oakley, Ph.D. author of *Learning How to Learn*, states: "A combination of feelings drives procrastination: a fear of failure, a lack of enjoyment, or simply feeling overwhelmed. But the key to overcoming procrastination lies in breaking tasks into manageable chunks and rewarding yourself for progress, no matter how small."

The procrastination cycle refers to a pattern of behavior where we consistently delay or avoid tasks we need to accomplish.

The Procrastination Cycle Typically Involves Several Stages:

1. **Task Avoidance:** The cycle begins with avoiding a specific task or set of tasks. This could be due to various reasons, including a lack of interest, feelings of overwhelm, fear of failure, or uncertainty about how to start.

2. **Short-Term Relief:** By avoiding the task, we often experience a short-term sense of relief or escape from the immediate stress or discomfort associated with the task.

3. **Increased Stress:** As time passes, the stress associated with the impending task increases. The awareness of the looming deadline or the consequences of not completing the task becomes more pronounced.

4. **Last-Minute Panic:** With the deadline approaching, we may enter a phase of last-minute panic. The pressure to complete the task becomes intense, leading to a flurry of activity in a short period.

5. **Completion (Sometimes):** In the final stage, the task is either completed hastily under stress, leading to potential suboptimal results, or it may not be completed at all, resulting in negative consequences.

6. **Relief or Regret:** Depending on whether the task was completed, we may experience a sense of relief if we managed to finish it or regret and anxiety if we did not.

The procrastination cycle is often perpetuated by negative emotions associated with the task, such as anxiety, fear, or boredom. It can become a habitual and chronic response to challenging or unpleasant tasks, leading to repeated procrastination. Breaking this cycle involves adopting strategies such as setting realistic goals, breaking tasks into smaller, manageable steps, addressing underlying issues, and cultivating a positive mindset towards work and deadlines.

Procrastination often isn't a matter of laziness—it's a response to fear, doubt, or the weight of perfectionism. When we delay, we usually avoid discomfort, not the task itself. True self-leadership begins when we confront the why behind our hesitation and take the first imperfect step forward.

Procrastination—Why We Do It

Procrastination is common, and people often have several reasons or excuses for putting off tasks or responsibilities. It is important to note that occasional procrastination is common and may not be a cause for concern. Addressing procrastination often involves developing better time management skills, setting clear goals, managing emotions, and breaking tasks into smaller, more manageable steps.

Common Excuses for Procrastination:

+ **Perfectionism:** We may hesitate to start a task or project because we want it to be perfect. We may fear making mistakes or being criticized, leading to procrastination.

+ **Irrational Delay:** Procrastination often involves unreasonable delay, where we delay tasks even when it is not in our best interest.

- **Lack of Motivation:** When we need more motivation or interest in a task, we may need help getting started or staying focused. Lack of motivation can lead to procrastination as we try to avoid the task.

- **Fear of Failure:** We may avoid starting a task or project because we fear not completing it successfully. This fear of failure can lead to procrastination as we try to avoid the negative emotions of disappointment.

- **Overwhelm:** When we feel overwhelmed by the scope or complexity of a task, we may need more time to avoid dealing with it.

- **Distractions:** In today's digital age, numerous distractions can distract us from our work or responsibilities. Social media, email, and other online distractions can make staying focused difficult and lead to procrastination.

- **Lack of Time Management Skills:** We may need help prioritizing tasks or managing our time effectively, leading to procrastination as we struggle to stay organized.

- **Lack of Accountability:** Without external accountability, we may find it easier to procrastinate as we do not feel we are answerable to anyone for our actions.

The Pomodoro Technique offers powerful benefits by turning time into a manageable, focused resource. Breaking tasks into short, structured intervals reduces burnout, enhances concentration, and makes overwhelming projects feel more achievable.

The Pomodoro Technique to Overcome Procrastination

The Pomodoro Technique is a time management method designed to boost productivity and overcome procrastination. Francesco Cirillo developed the technique in the late 1980s. The Pomodoro is named after the Italian word for 'tomato' due to the tomato-shaped kitchen timer Cirillo initially used.

The Pomodoro technique aims to improve productivity through a simple process. Its goals include reducing anxiety, improving focus by minimizing interruptions, increasing awareness of decisions, boosting motivation, and refining goal estimation processes. Additionally, it aims to enhance work or study processes, strengthen determination in complex situations, and foster a determined approach to achieving one's qualitative and quantitative goals.

How the Pomodoro Technique Works:

- **Choose a Task**: Start by selecting a task you want to work on. It can be any work-related, studying, writing, or personal task.

- **Set a Timer**: Set a timer for twenty-five minutes, which is one Pomodoro. During this time, focus exclusively on the chosen task and work diligently.

- **Work on the Task**: Concentrate on the task and work as efficiently as possible. Avoid distractions and interruptions.

- **Complete the Pomodoro**: When the timer rings after twenty-five minutes, stop working on the task, even if you are in the middle of something. This marks the completion of one Pomodoro.

- **Take a Short Break**: Take a five-minute rest and recharge. Stretch, grab a drink, or step away from your work area.

- **Repeat**: Repeat steps one to five for the same task. After completing four Pomodoros, take a more extended break of fifteen-thirty minutes.

To Adapt the Pomodoro Technique to Your Needs:

+ Adjust the Pomodoro length if twenty-five minutes is too short or long for you.

+ Use a timer, app, or Pomodoro-specific software to track your work intervals and breaks.

+ Experiment with the number of Pomodoros you complete daily based on your energy levels and workload.

Procrastination—The Why and Root Cause— Insular Cortex and Neuroscience

Procrastination is a complex behavior with various underlying causes. The insular cortex, a region deep within the brain, has been linked to certain aspects of procrastination. The insular cortex is involved in processing emotions, self-awareness, and decision-making.

Procrastination Neuroscience and Causes:

+ **Emotional Regulation:** The insular cortex regulates emotions. Procrastination often involves negative emotions like anxiety, fear, or even guilt, which the anticipation of a task can trigger. When these negative emotions become overwhelming, they can lead to avoidance behavior, contributing to procrastination.

+ **Self-Awareness:** The insular cortex is associated with self-awareness and self-reflection. Procrastinators may engage in self-criticism or negative self-talk, which can be linked to the insular cortex's function. Self-awareness can also lead to realizing the consequences of procrastination, which may motivate you to overcome it.

+ **Decision-Making:** Procrastination is deciding whether to delay or avoid a task. The insular cortex is involved in decision-making processes, including evaluating the costs and benefits of different actions. Procrastinators may struggle with deciding when and how to start a task, and the insular cortex may play a role in this decision-making process.

+ **Task Salience:** The insular cortex helps determine the salience or importance of tasks. Procrastinators may find it challenging to prioritize tasks, often delaying important ones in favor of less important or more immediately rewarding activities. The insular cortex's involvement in assessing task salience may contribute to this issue.

+ **Fear of Failure:** Promotes procrastination primarily when it reduces our sense of autonomy or when we feel incapable of dealing with a task; we are afraid of failing.

+ **People Feel Overwhelmed:** Avoiding the task at hand seems easier to avoid the uncomfortable state of mind.

It is important to note that while the insular cortex has been associated with procrastination, it is just one part of a complex neural network involved in this behavior. Cognitive, emotional, and motivational factors influence procrastination. Understanding these factors and developing strategies to address them can help you overcome procrastination, whether or not the insular cortex plays a significant role in their specific case.

Dr. Barbara Oakley exemplifies how overcoming procrastination starts with understanding how your brain works. By breaking tasks into manageable steps and staying consistent, she transformed her learning journey and now empowers others to do the same.

Barbara Oakley–Author of *Learning How to Learn*– Story On Overcoming Procrastination

Barbara Oakley, the author of *Learning How to Learn*, is a prominent example of someone who has overcome procrastination. Early in her life, she struggled with learning and often procrastinated, particularly in math and engineering. Despite these challenges, Oakley eventually became a professor of engineering at Oakland University and a leading voice in cognitive psychology.

Her journey from procrastination to mastery began when she recognized the importance of mindset and practical strategies for overcoming mental hurdles. Oakley employed techniques such as breaking tasks into smaller, manageable chunks, using the Pomodoro Technique to maintain focus in short bursts, and learning to switch between "focused" and "diffuse" modes of thinking—two cognitive processes the brain uses to solve problems.

Through her experiences, Oakley discovered that the habits and mindset shifts that helped her conquer procrastination were beneficial for her personal growth and others. This realization inspired her to write *Learning How to Learn*, where she shares research-based strategies that aided her, including methods to combat procrastination, develop effective study habits, and foster a growth mindset.

Oakley's story illustrates that overcoming procrastination is not merely about willpower; it involves understanding how the brain functions and applying practical techniques to work smarter, not harder.

External Interruptions

External interruptions can significantly disrupt productivity and focus. External interruptions, such as email and phone calls, can substantially disrupt focus and productivity by demanding immediate attention.

Open computer windows can also distract our focus from meaningful work, as new requests take precedence over long-term activities. Someone often initiates these interruptions, whether a colleague with an urgent request or a supervisor needing immediate input.

A distracting environment and the knowledge that someone is waiting for a response can exacerbate the problem. Additionally, external interruptions can occur when others impose their tasks or priorities on us, diverting our attention from our planned activities. Managing these external interruptions is essential for maintaining productivity and accomplishing long-term goals.

Common Examples of External Interruptions:

+ **Phone Calls:** Incoming calls on a mobile or office phone can interrupt work and divert attention.

+ **Emails and Notifications:** Pop-up notifications, email alerts, or constant updates from messaging apps can break concentration.

+ **Office Noise:** Background noise in a shared workspace, such as conversations, ringing phones, or office equipment, can be distracting.

- **Meetings and Discussions:** Unscheduled or frequent meetings can disrupt workflow and require shifting focus away from current tasks.

- **Visitors and Drop-Ins:** Colleagues or visitors stopping by without prior notice can interrupt work and demand immediate attention.

- **Environmental Disturbances:** External factors like construction noise, sirens, or other environmental disturbances can disrupt concentration.

- **Technology Issues:** Technical problems, such as computer crashes or network failures, can interrupt work and require troubleshooting.

- **Social Media:** Notifications from social media platforms can be distracting, primarily when focusing on work.

- **Unexpected Events:** Unforeseen emergencies, fire alarms, or other sudden disruptions can interrupt daily activities.

Internal Interruptions

Internal interruptions, originating within our minds, can be just as disruptive to our concentration and productivity. These interruptions often manifest as pain signals emanating from the insular cortex, causing discomfort and diverting our attention from the task at hand. Internal negative dialogues, self-doubt, or a wandering mind can lead our thoughts astray, convincing us to shift our focus elsewhere. Sometimes, our inner voice suggests alternative activities or makes us believe that the current task is too complex or redundant.

The fear of making mistakes or facing criticism can also be a source of internal interruption, as can the pressure to achieve perfection and evaluate multiple alternatives. Additionally, when faced with an overwhelming number of choices, internal interruptions can give rise to anxiety and hinder our ability to stay focused on our intended activities. Managing and mitigating these internal interruptions is crucial for maintaining productivity and mental clarity.

Internal interruptions are distractions or disruptions that originate within you and interfere with your focus or attention on a specific task or activity. These interruptions often involve mental processes, thoughts, or habits that divert attention from the present task.

Common Examples of Internal Interruptions:

+ **Mind Wandering:** The mind drifting away from the current task to unrelated thoughts or daydreams can interrupt concentration.

+ **Lack of Focus:** Difficulty maintaining sustained attention on a task due to restlessness or boredom can be internally disruptive.

+ **Procrastination:** Delaying or postponing tasks instead of working on them can be a significant internal interruption.

+ **Negative Self-Talk:** Inner criticism or negative self-talk can undermine confidence and disrupt a positive and focused mindset.

+ **Multitasking:** Trying to juggle multiple tasks simultaneously can lead to internal interruptions as attention is divided among different activities.

+ **Stress and Anxiety:** Mental stress, anxiety, or worrying about unrelated issues can interfere with concentration and focus.

+ **Perfectionism:** Striving for perfection and being overly critical of one's work can lead to interruptions and delays.

+ **Impulsivity:** Acting on impulses or distractions without considering the impact on the current task can interrupt workflow.

+ **Lack of Clarity:** Unclear goals or a lack of direction can lead to internal interruptions as you struggle to define your priorities.

+ **Overthinking:** Analyzing a task excessively or getting caught up in details can lead to overthinking, disrupting the workflow.

Managing internal interruptions involves developing self-awareness and adopting strategies to address cognitive and emotional factors that contribute to distractions. Techniques such as mindfulness, goal setting, time management, and addressing underlying stressors can help minimize internal interruptions and enhance focus and productivity.

The 2-Minute Rule is a powerful tool for managing time and tasks efficiently. By quickly addressing small actions, you clear your mental and physical workspace, making it easier to focus on larger goals and maintain steady progress throughout the day.

The 2-Minute Rule, popularized by David Allen in his productivity book "Getting Things Done," is a simple but effective strategy to increase efficiency and reduce procrastination. The rule states that if a task can be completed in two minutes or less, you should do it immediately rather than postponing it.

My Story—Managing Internal Interruptions

Managing my internal interruptions is challenging and often frustrating, especially when setting goals and overcoming the mindless chatter in my mind. My mind can incessantly chatter about thoughts and feelings that can interfere with the rational goal-setting part of my mind. Many times, I struggle to overcome this part of my internal interruptions. I call this state 'I am in the crazy car.' I use this phrase to laugh at myself and my thoughts. I find this lessens the impact of my internal interruptions.

To counteract these internal interruptions, I have utilized the following tools and techniques:

- **Mindful Meditation:** Mindful meditation techniques to quiet the chatter that can go on in my mind. I significantly change my state of mind and disrupt internal interruptions by focusing on my breathing.

- **Pomodoro Technique:** This helps me overcome my initial inertia to complete tasks. This tool disrupts my negative thinking patterns so I can concentrate on the task at hand. The Pomodoro technique and habit help me to overcome internal interruptions.

- **Box Breathing:** This technique helps me get out of my head and the chatter in my mind.

- **Journaling:** I write down my thoughts and feelings in a journal so I can identify and manage my thoughts and feelings. Writing down my thoughts and feelings gets me out of my head and disrupts negative thoughts or feelings.

- **Getting Sleep:** Getting plenty of sleep helps me focus on my goals and tasks needed to get tasks done and goals accomplished.

- **Toxic People:** I do my best to stay away from toxic people, and at the most, I keep a physical distance to stay out of 'the crazy car.'

In summary, I use tools and techniques to handle the internal interruptions. This helps me develop habits to overcome internal disruption. These methods have helped me significantly.

You, too, can manage the internal interruptions in our minds. Write down a few tools and techniques you can utilize to manage them.

Overcoming procrastination unlocks your potential, turning hesitation into progress. It empowers you to control your time, focus on your goals, and build the momentum needed to achieve lasting success.

Summary

The Pomodoro Technique offers a valuable method to overcome procrastination. It is a simple and effective way to cultivate a growth mindset and combat its impact.

The Two-Minute Rule is a powerful tool for managing time and tasks efficiently. By quickly addressing small actions, you clear your mental and physical workspace, making it easier to focus on larger goals and maintain steady progress throughout the day.

Procrastination is the thief of time and the enemy of progress. To conquer it, we must summon the courage to face discomfort, embrace discipline, and take relentless action toward one's goals. For in the battle against procrastination lies the key to unlocking the door to success.

Overcoming procrastination requires a combination of self-awareness, effective time management strategies, and behavioral changes. It involves identifying the underlying reasons for procrastination, such as fear of failure, perfectionism, or lack of motivation, and addressing them through cognitive restructuring and self-reflection.

Understanding goals and priorities is essential to combat procrastination, break tasks into smaller, manageable steps, and set deadlines. You can foster a proactive mindset and increase productivity by implementing strategies such as the Pomodoro Technique and the Two-Minute Rule, creating a conducive work environment, and practicing self-discipline.

By cultivating self-awareness, employing effective time management techniques, and implementing behavioral changes, you can overcome procrastination and achieve your goals more efficiently and successfully.

Action Plan

By following this action plan, you can gradually build better habits, reduce procrastination, and increase your productivity and sense of accomplishment.

1. Identify the root causes of procrastination, such as fear of failure, perfectionism, lack of interest, or feeling overwhelmed.

2. Create a schedule and use tools like calendars, planners, or apps to stay organized.

3. Eliminate distractions by finding a quiet workspace and using the Pomodoro Technique.

4. Implement the Two-Minute Rule to tackle small tasks immediately.

5. Reward yourself for completing tasks and stay accountable by sharing your goals with someone.

6. Practice self-compassion and regularly review your progress to make necessary adjustments.

7. Regularly review your progress and identify what strategies are working or need adjustment.

8. Make changes to your action plan as needed to stay on track.

9. If you can complete a task in two minutes, do it.

CHAPTER 9

Developing SMART Habits

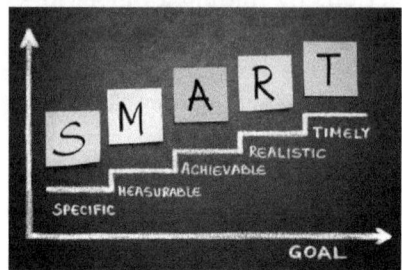

"Habit is either the best of servants or the worst of masters."

—Seneca—Roman Stoic philosopher

Developing SMART Habits

Developing SMART habits is the cornerstone of personal growth and achievement, empowering you to take control of your journey. By intentionally cultivating routines and behaviors that align with your goals and values, you consistently empower yourself to progress toward success. SMART habits are not only about what you do but also about how you do it. They involve active mindfulness, discipline, and self-awareness, enabling us to break free from autopilot mode and take deliberate action. Through small, incremental changes, you create lasting transformations in our lives, unlocking our full potential and paving the way for a brighter future. With dedication and perseverance, you can turn your aspirations into reality and live a life of purpose and fulfillment.

Habits are the routines and behaviors that shape your daily life, influencing your actions and decisions. SMART habits are intentional and positive behaviors that contribute to your well-being and personal growth. While establishing habits is a powerful way to enhance your life, various obstacles can impede your progress. These obstacles may include a lack of motivation, environmental triggers, or the challenge of breaking existing habits. Overcoming these obstacles involves a strategic approach, starting with setting specific and achievable goals for habit formation.

Creating a supportive environment, identifying and addressing triggers, and seeking accountability from friends or family are effective strategies. However, it is not just about the strategy but the journey. Celebrating small wins and learning from setbacks are crucial parts of the process. They contribute to the resilience needed for habit development. Understanding the definition of habits, focusing on SMART habits, and actively addressing obstacles can pave the way for positive and lasting life changes.

SMART Habits Defined

Developing SMART habits offers significant benefits that can transform your personal and professional life. By ensuring that your habits are Specific, Measurable, Achievable, Relevant, and Time-bound, you create a clear roadmap for success. These structured habits provide focus and direction, making staying committed and tracking progress easier. The clarity and precision of SMART habits help eliminate ambiguity, allowing you to make steady, intentional progress toward your goals. Additionally, because they are designed to be realistic and aligned with your broader objectives, SMART habits are more sustainable and likely to lead to lasting change. By cultivating SMART habits, you build a foundation for continuous improvement, increased productivity, and long-term achievement.

Developing SMART habits starts with intentionality and consistency. It's about making small, manageable changes that compound over time. The key is to focus on what truly matters and align those habits with your long-term goals, creating a foundation for sustained growth and success.

SMART Habit Framework:

+   **Specific:** The habit should be clear and well-defined. Instead of saying, "I want to exercise," a specific habit would be "I will do thirty minutes of cardio every morning."

+   **Measurable:** The habit should have a quantifiable outcome so you can track progress. For example, "I will drink eight glasses of water daily" is measurable.

+   **Achievable:** The habit should be realistic and attainable within your current lifestyle. For instance, if you're new to meditation, starting with "I will meditate for five minutes each day" is more achievable than aiming for an hour.

+   **Relevant:** The habit should align with your long-term goals and values. For example, "I will read for twenty minutes each night" is relevant if your goal is to increase knowledge or reduce screen time before bed.

+   **Time-bound:** The habit should have a specific timeframe, creating urgency and focus. An example would be, "I will go for a ten-minute walk after lunch every day."

By applying the SMART criteria to habits, you ensure that they are structured to increase the likelihood of consistency and success, ultimately leading to meaningful and lasting change.

SMART habits are built on consistency, simplicity, and alignment with your goals. Start small, pair new habits with existing routines, and track your progress. The key is to make the habit so practical and rewarding that it becomes second nature.

Practical Ways to Develop SMART Habits

Developing SMART habits involves incorporating intentional, positive behaviors into your daily routine. Smart habits contribute to your overall well-being, productivity, and long-term goals.

Ways to Develop SMART Habits:

- **Start Small:** Begin with tiny, manageable habits. Starting small makes integrating them into your routine more accessible and increases the likelihood of success.

- **Be Specific:** Clearly define your habit. Instead of a vague goal like "exercise more," specify "take a twenty-minute walk every morning." Specificity provides clarity and a clear action plan.

- **Attach Habits to Existing Cues:** Associate new habits with existing cues or routines. For example, if you want to establish a habit of stretching, link it to brushing your teeth each morning.

- **Use Triggers:** Identify triggers that prompt your habit. This could be a time of day, a specific event, or an environmental cue. Utilize these triggers to remind yourself to perform the habit.

+ **Create a Routine:** Establish a consistent routine. Habits thrive on consistency, so try to perform your habit simultaneously or in the same context each day.

+ **Track Your Progress:** Record your habit-forming journey. Tracking your progress provides a sense of accomplishment and helps you stay accountable.

+ **Accountability Partners:** Share your habit goals with a friend, family member, or colleague who can support and hold you accountable. Having someone to share your progress with adds motivation.

+ **Celebrate Small Wins:** Celebrate your achievements, no matter how small. Recognizing progress boosts motivation and reinforces the habit loop.

+ **Visual Reminders:** Place visual reminders in your environment. This could be a sticky note on your mirror or a digital reminder on your phone. Visual cues prompt you to remember and execute your habit.

+ **Practice Patience:** Habits take time to develop. Be patient and persistent, especially during the initial stages when the habit is not yet ingrained.

+ **Incorporate Habits into Goals:** Align your habits with broader goals. Connecting habits to meaningful objectives enhances motivation and provides a sense of purpose.

+ **Focus on Keystone Habits:** Identify keystone habits, small changes that can cascade positive effects on other areas of your life. Working on keystone habits can lead to broader improvements.

+ **Learn from Setbacks:** If you encounter setbacks, view them as learning opportunities. Analyze what went wrong, adjust your approach, and refine your habits.

- **Adapt as Needed:** Be flexible and willing to adapt your habits. Life circumstances may change, and your habits should be sustainable in different situations.

- **Reflect Regularly:** Set aside time for reflection. Assess your habits, evaluate their impact, and adjust as needed. Regular reflection enhances self-awareness and aids in continuous improvement.

By incorporating these strategies into your habit-forming process, you can increase the likelihood of success and make positive, lasting changes in your life.

SMART Habit Examples

Developing SMART habits is not just a choice. Achieving positive changes in various areas of your life, including productivity, health, personal growth, and overall well-being, is necessary. The journey requires dedication and perseverance, but the rewards are immense.

Examples of SMART Habits:

- **Time Management:** Effective time management involves prioritizing tasks, setting goals, and utilizing productivity techniques like the Pomodoro Technique. Creating to-do lists and minimizing distractions are essential steps in improving time management.

- **Regular Exercise:** To maintain good health, we must include physical activity in our daily routines, dedicate time for workouts, and choose enjoyable and sustainable activities.

+ **Healthy Eating:** To maintain a healthy body and improve mental well-being, it is crucial to plan and prepare meals ahead of time, opt for whole foods instead of processed ones, and regulate portion sizes. These SMART habits are vital for ensuring that the body receives the necessary nutrients.

+ **Continuous Learning:** Engaging in activities such as reading books, attending seminars or workshops, and seeking new experiences and perspectives are vital for personal growth and professional development.

+ **Setting Goals:** It is crucial to have well-defined goals, break them down into manageable steps, and regularly assess progress to boost motivation and maintain focus.

+ **Daily Reflection:** Journaling, practicing mindfulness or meditation, and actively seeking feedback from others are essential for achieving self-awareness and personal growth. These practices are non-negotiable.

+ **Financial Management:** It is essential to cultivate intelligent financial habits such as budgeting, saving money, and removing unnecessary debt. Creating a comprehensive financial plan for the long term and keeping track of expenses are crucial steps toward achieving this goal.

+ **Effective Communication:** To effectively communicate, it is crucial to actively listen, express thoughts clearly and respectfully, and seek understanding before responding. These skills are vital and should take precedence in any conversation.

+ **Organization and Decluttering:** Consistent decluttering, effective organization methods, and cleanliness in your living space are essential practices that can alleviate stress and enhance productivity.

+ **Self-Care:** Prioritizing sufficient sleep, incorporating relaxation practices, pursuing enjoyable hobbies, and seeking out support from others are essential for maintaining optimal well-being.

It is essential to keep in mind that forming smart habits is a process that requires patience and consistency. Make small, attainable changes and gradually integrate them into your daily routine. Over time, these habits can enhance various aspects of your life.

Warren Buffett's approach to developing SMART habits is rooted in simplicity and focus. By prioritizing a few critical tasks and saying no to distractions, he exemplifies how consistency in the right actions can compound into extraordinary results over time.

Warren Buffet—Developing SMART Habits

One well-known example of a famous person developing SMART habits is Warren Buffett, the legendary investor and CEO of Berkshire Hathaway. Buffett is renowned for his investment acumen and disciplined approach to life and work, which revolves around developing smart habits that contribute to his long-term success.

Warren Buffett's Story of Developing Smart Habits:

1. **Habit of Reading:**
   - Buffett's 'Five-Hour Rule': Buffett famously spends five to six hours a day reading and has maintained this habit throughout his life. He believes that acquiring knowledge through constant reading is one of the keys to making informed decisions. This habit of continuous learning gives him an edge in business and investing.
   - He once advised, "Read 500 pages like this every day. That's how knowledge works. It builds up, like compound interest." This daily habit has helped him stay ahead by continuously broadening his knowledge base.

2. **Discipline and Focus on Essentials:**
    *   Buffett developed the habit of focusing on what truly matters. Early in his career, he learned the importance of prioritizing. One of his famous habits is the 'twenty-slot rule', which means you should act as if you have only twenty investment opportunities over your lifetime. This forces him to think long and hard before committing to anything, ensuring that he focuses only on high-impact actions.
    *   This SMART habit is applied not just to his investment strategy but to his general life philosophy, keeping a narrow focus on the most critical goals and ignoring distractions.

3. **Avoiding Bad Habits:**
    *   Buffett has also discussed how avoiding bad habits is just as important as developing good ones. He's said bad habits are like chains that are too light to feel until they're too heavy to break. He advises against habits like procrastination, unnecessary spending, or emotional decision-making.

4. **Consistency and Long-Term Thinking:**
    *   Buffett cultivated the habit of long-term thinking. He doesn't chase trends or get swept up in fads. Instead, he invests in companies he believes will have long-term value, even unpopular ones. His patience and consistency in sticking to this habit have led to decades of success in the stock market.
    *   Buffett's story shows how SMART habits—like disciplined reading, prioritization, avoiding bad habits, and long-term thinking—can lead to extraordinary success. His habits help him stay informed, focused, and ahead of the competition in a field where long-term success is rare.

Obstacles To SMART Habits

Obstacles can hinder progress and challenge one's determination, whether due to a busy routine, unexpected setbacks, or inner resistance. Several factors and obstacles can prevent habit development. These challenges can vary from person to person and situation to situation.

Common Obstacles That Hinder the Development of SMART Habits:

- **Lack of Motivation:** When you lack a strong reason or motivation to establish a habit, it is challenging to stay committed.

- **Lack of Clarity:** Unclear goals or a lack of understanding about why a habit is essential can hinder progress.

- **Overwhelm:** Establishing too many habits at once can be overwhelming and unsustainable.

- **Lack of Consistency:** Inconsistent effort can prevent habits from becoming ingrained in your routine.

- **Lack of Accountability:** It is easy to stray from your habits without someone to hold you accountable.

- **Negative Self-Talk:** Negative thoughts and self-doubt can discourage you from sticking to your habits.

- **Lack of Patience:** Habits take time to develop, and impatience can lead to giving up too soon.

+ **External Influences:** Environmental factors, such as a lack of resources or support, can impede habit formation.

+ **Stress and Life Changes:** Major life changes or high-stress levels can disrupt your efforts to establish habits.

+ **Fear of Failure:** The fear of failing or making mistakes can prevent you from even attempting to develop habits.

+ **Unrealistic Expectations:** Setting overly ambitious goals can lead to frustration and demotivation.

+ **Lack of Routine:** Inconsistent daily routines can make it challenging to incorporate new habits.

+ **Distractions:** Constant distractions and lack of focus can interfere with habit-building efforts.

+ **Lack of Positive Reinforcement:** It can be hard to stay committed if you do not see positive results or rewards from your habits.

+ **Old Patterns:** Breaking away from old, ingrained patterns and replacing them with new habits can be challenging.

Overcoming these obstacles requires self-awareness, strategy, and perseverance. Addressing these challenges, seeking support, and focusing on your goals can increase your chances of successfully developing new habits.

"There are only two days in the year that nothing can be done. One is called yesterday, and the other is called tomorrow, so today is the right day to love, believe, do, and mostly live."

Dalai Lama—Tibetan Buddhist Monk

Now vs. Later Thinking

'Now vs. Later Thinking' refers to the cognitive approach when making decisions, considering the immediate gratification of the present moment versus the potential long-term benefits or consequences. This concept is often associated with the psychological concept of time preference, which influences how people weigh the value of rewards or outcomes at different points in time.

Key aspects of 'Now vs. Later Thinking':

+ **Immediate Gratification:** Individuals with a 'Now' mindset prioritize immediate rewards or pleasures. They might choose options that bring instant satisfaction, even if there are potential negative consequences in the future.

+ **Delayed Gratification:** On the other hand, with a 'Later' mindset, we are willing to postpone immediate rewards in favor of greater benefits or rewards in the future. This involves the ability to resist impulsive choices for the sake of long-term goals.

- **Impulsivity vs. Patience:** 'Now' thinking is associated with impulsivity, where decisions are made based on immediate desires. 'Later' thinking involves patience, discipline, and the ability to delay rewards for a more significant payoff later.

- **Financial Decision-Making:** In personal finance, 'Now vs. Later Thinking' influences spending versus saving. Individuals inclined toward 'Now' thinking may spend impulsively, while those favoring 'Later' thinking may prioritize saving for future goals.

- **Health and Lifestyle Choices:** This mindset is evident in health-related decisions. Choosing between indulging in unhealthy foods for immediate pleasure or a nutritious diet for long-term well-being reflects 'Now vs. Later Thinking.'

- **Educational and Career Choices:** In education and career planning, we might face decisions that involve sacrificing short-term comfort for long-term success. Those with a 'Later' mindset may prioritize education and skill-building for future career prospects.

- **Risk-Taking Behavior:** Risk-taking behavior can be influenced by time preference. 'Now' thinkers may engage in risky behaviors for immediate excitement, while 'Later' thinkers may avoid such behaviors for long-term safety and well-being.

- **Goal Setting:** 'Now vs. Later Thinking' is integral to goal setting. With a 'Later' mindset, we are more likely to set and work towards long-term goals, while 'Now' thinkers may struggle to pursue objectives that yield delayed rewards consistently.

Understanding and managing this cognitive bias is essential for making informed decisions aligning with one's values, goals, and well-being. Striking a balance between immediate gratification and long-term planning is critical to achieving a harmonious and fulfilling life.

My Story—SMART Habits—Riding A Bike—Four Times a Week

Developing the SMART habit of riding a bike every morning at 5:00 a.m. is an excellent way to start my day with energy and focus. This early morning routine allows me to enjoy the quiet and peaceful atmosphere before the world wakes up, making it a perfect time for reflection and mental clarity. Consistently riding at this time helps me to build discipline and sets a positive tone for the rest of the day. Physical activity boosts my fitness and enhances my mood and productivity throughout the day. Over time, this habit strengthens my body, sharpens my mind, and becomes a rewarding and energizing start each morning.

Specifics of the SMART Habit:

1. **S—Specific**
   - Four mornings a week
   - I wake up at 5:00 am.
   - Make a cup of coffee.
   - Put on my workout clothes.

2. **M—Measurable:**
   - I will ride my bike for sixty minutes four times weekly.
   - Minimum heart rate of eighty-five beats per minute.

3. **A—Achievable:**
   - Started at thirty minutes a day, then increased to forty-five minutes, then to sixty minutes four times a week.

4. **R—Relevant:**
   - Improved health and stamina.
   - Weight loss
   - Improved mental health.
   - Improved energy.

5. **T—Time-bound:**
   - I will bike every day between 5:00 a.m. and 7:00 am.

SMART habits are the building blocks of success.
You transform small actions into powerful results over
time by creating intentional routines, aligning them
with your goals, and consistently practicing them.

Summary

Developing smart habits offers many benefits that can positively impact your life. Smart habits, characterized by consistency, intentionality, and effectiveness, contribute to enhanced productivity, improved time management, and increased efficiency in daily activities. By cultivating SMART habits, you can streamline your routines, reduce decision fatigue, and optimize your use of time and resources. Furthermore, SMART habits promote personal growth and self-improvement by fostering discipline, resilience, and goal-oriented behavior.

Over time, these SMART habits become ingrained and lead to long-term positive outcomes, including improved health and well-being, enhanced performance in academic and professional endeavors, and greater overall satisfaction and fulfillment in life. Ultimately, developing smart habits empowers you to make deliberate choices, achieve your goals, and live a more purposeful and fulfilling life.

Embrace the power of a growth mindset, and develop SMART habits where challenges are opportunities, setbacks are stepping stones, and every effort fuels your journey toward greatness.

Action Plan

Following this action plan can help you develop smart habits to enhance your productivity, well-being, and overall success.

1. **Define Your Goals**
   + Identify specific habits and set achievable goals.
   + Write them down in a workbook or a journal.

2. **Start Small**
   + Begin with manageable steps to build consistency.
   + Chunk your steps into smaller steps and activities.

3. **Create a Routine**
   + Integrate the new habit into your daily routine.
   + Have a specific place and time.

4. **Use Reminders and Triggers**
   + Set reminders and identify triggers for the habit.
   + Write down your triggers and reactions.

5. **Track Your Progress**
   + Use a habit tracker and celebrate small wins.
   + Develop a spreadsheet, calendar, or tools to track your progress.

6. **Stay Consistent**
   + Aim for consistency and practice the habit daily.
   + Try to develop a habit of achieving your goals.

7. **Adjust as Needed**
   + Reflect on what is working and adjust.
   + Expect roadblocks and frustrations.

8. **Find Accountability**
   + Share your goals and consider joining a community.
   + Consider working with a role model or mentor.

9. **Reward Yourself**
   + Establish a reward system to reinforce positive behavior.
   + Develop a list of rewards you can use.

10. **Be Patient and Persistent**
    + Understand that developing new habits takes time.
    + Be mindful that each step or activity moves you toward your goals.

CHAPTER 10

SMART Networking for Personal and Professional Success

"The currency of real networking is not greed but generosity."

Keith Ferrazzi—*Never Eat Alone*

SMART Connections and Networks

Developing relationships and connections with others is vital to your personal and professional success. It can significantly enhance your chances in both your professional and personal life. Networking is meaningful relationships built on trust, mutual respect, and a willingness to help each other. It is not just about exchanging business cards or making superficial connections but about cultivating a strong network, which can provide a wealth of knowledge, opportunities, and resources to facilitate personal and professional growth.

Developing networking skills can help you gain valuable insights, discover new opportunities, and build mutually beneficial relationships. It consists of interacting with people, exchanging information, and creating a network of contacts that can help achieve personal and career objectives. Building a diverse network involves connecting with people from different backgrounds, industries, and areas of expertise. This can be accomplished by attending professional events, industry conferences, social gatherings, online platforms, and seeking referrals. Expanding your network can bring fresh perspectives, new ideas, and unexpected opportunities.

Networking requires a genuine approach. Rather than considering it solely for self-benefit, focusing on how to add value and contribute to others is crucial. Listen attentively, show interest in their experiences, and support their endeavors. By building a reputation for being dependable and trustworthy, you will become a valuable resource and attract like-minded individuals who may become lifelong connections. This can be accomplished by attending professional events, industry conferences, social gatherings, online platforms, and seeking referrals.

Expand your connections and discover the endless opportunities that personal networking can bring. It can lead to career growth, mentoring, and even personal development. Building a network can significantly impact your future, so why not start today and experience the power of networking? Remember that networking is an ongoing effort that demands time and energy to create opportunities. The key is cultivating and maintaining connections, following up on leads, and proactively providing help and support whenever possible.

Business and Professional Networking

A business and professional network is a *social network* whose reason for existing is business networking activity. Many business people contend that business networking is a more cost-effective method of generating new business than advertising or public relations efforts. This is because business networking is a low-cost activity that involves more personal commitment than company money. Business networking can be conducted in a local business community or on a larger scale via the Internet.

Many businesses use networking as a critical factor in their marketing plan. It helps develop a strong trust between those involved and plays a big part in raising a company's profile and products. Suppliers and businesses can be seen as networked businesses. They tend to source the business and their suppliers through their relationships with the companies they work closely with. Networked businesses tend to be open, random, and supportive, whereas those relying on hierarchical, traditionally managed approaches are closed, selective, and controlling.

Business networking websites, i.e., LinkedIn, have grown over recent years due to the Internet's ability to connect businesspeople worldwide. Internet businesses often set up business leads for sale to corporations and businesses looking for data sources for business. Before online business networking, face-to-face business networking existed. Several techniques, such as trade show marketing and loyalty programs, achieved this. Though these techniques have been proven to be an effective source of income, many companies now focus more on online marketing due to the ability to track every detail of a campaign and justify the spending involved in setting up one of these campaigns. 'Schmoozing' or 'rubbing elbows' are expressions used among business professionals to introduce and meet one another in a business context and establish business rapport.

In the case of a formal business network, its members may agree to meet weekly or monthly to exchange business leads and referrals with fellow members. To complement this business activity, members often meet outside this circle, on their own time, and build their one-to-one business relationships with fellow members.

Trust is the foundation of every successful network.
It transforms connections into collaborations and turns
opportunities into lasting partnerships. Without trust,
a network is just a collection of names.

Building Trust

Trust is crucial for developing strong connections and cooperation in personal and professional relationships. Trust is the foundation of positive interactions, creating a secure and valued environment where people feel confident. To build trust, one should prioritize transparent communication, consistent actions, and a genuine commitment to understanding and respecting others' perspectives. Demonstrating reliability, empathy, and the ability to admit mistakes contributes to gradually building a trustworthy and dependable foundation. Building trust is a continuous process that requires dedication, integrity, and a shared commitment to nurturing relationships based on mutual respect and understanding.

Benefits of SMART Connections and Networks

Building personal and professional connections provides numerous benefits.

Advantages of Personal and Professional Networking:

+ **Opportunities:** Building a solid network is crucial for expanding your horizons and finding fresh opportunities. Connecting with people from different backgrounds increases your chances of stumbling upon job prospects, establishing business partnerships, fostering collaborations, gaining mentors, and exploring avenues for personal and professional development.

+ **Knowledge and Insights:** Networking can be a valuable opportunity to gain insights and perspectives from others. Conversing and interacting with individuals from diverse backgrounds and industries can provide useful knowledge, industry developments, optimal approaches, and diverse outlooks to expand your knowledge and proficiency.

+ **Support and Guidance:** A strong network can provide a dependable support system. It allows you to get helpful advice, mentorship, and guidance from people who have encountered similar challenges or have knowledge in areas that interest you. Surrounding yourself with supportive individuals can give you motivation, encouragement, and valuable insights to assist you in your personal or professional endeavors.

- **Increased Visibility:** Attending networking events and interacting with fellow professionals in your field can enhance your visibility and set you apart. Building a reputation within your professional community improves your prospects of being acknowledged and memorable to others. Such heightened exposure can lead to promising opportunities, partnerships, or recommendations.

- **Collaboration and Partnerships:** Networking is vital in establishing collaborations and partnerships. Consider joint ventures, collaborative projects, and partnerships that enhance your work or business opportunities. Additionally, networking is an efficient method for identifying potential clients, customers, or suppliers.

- **Personal Development:** Participating in networking can be a valuable opportunity for personal development. Communicating with others, sharing ideas, and receiving helpful feedback can enhance your communication skills, expand your knowledge, and gain fresh perspectives. Additionally, networking can boost your confidence and improve your ability to form connections.

- **Access to Resources:** Building a strong network can provide numerous benefits and opportunities. It can offer access to valuable information, industry connections, financing options, or specialized knowledge. The people in your network might be willing to share their resources or introduce you to others who can assist you in achieving your goals.

- **Social and Emotional Support:** Establishing connections with people who share common interests can offer invaluable emotional and social assistance, creating a feeling of unity and inclusion. Additionally, this can lead to the discovery of mentors, companions, and colleagues who have gone through similar obstacles and can provide support, sympathy, and a sense of belonging. Remember that networking should be a mutually beneficial exchange, so giving back to others is just as crucial.

Strategies to Develop SMART Networks and Alliances

Developing SMART networks and alliances is crucial for personal and professional growth. We expand our opportunities, knowledge, and support system by strategically building relationships with like-minded individuals, mentors, and collaborators. SMART networks are not just about the quantity of connections but also the quality. It is about fostering genuine, mutually beneficial relationships built on trust, respect, and reciprocity. Through these networks, we gain access to valuable resources, insights, and opportunities that can propel us forward in our endeavors. Additionally, we enhance our creativity, innovation, and problem-solving abilities by surrounding ourselves with diverse perspectives and expertise. SMART networks and alliances catalyze success, enabling us to achieve our goals and thrive in an ever-changing world.

Personal Networking Strategies to Build and Leverage Your Personal and Professional Network:

* **Set Networking Goals:** Define clear objectives for networking, such as expanding your professional contacts, seeking career advice, or exploring new job opportunities. Setting specific goals will guide your networking efforts and help you focus on achieving tangible outcomes.

- **Attend Networking Events:** Participating in networking events, conferences, seminars, and workshops relevant to your industry or field is an exciting opportunity. These events provide chances to meet new people, exchange ideas, and build relationships with professionals in your interest, igniting your enthusiasm for networking.

- **Utilize Online Networking Platforms:** Leverage online networking platforms such as LinkedIn, professional association websites, and industry-specific forums to connect with professionals, join relevant groups, and engage in discussions. Use these platforms to highlight your expertise, share insights, and connect with like-minded individuals.

- **Join Professional Associations:** Becoming a member of professional associations, trade organizations, or alumni groups related to your field is a way to belong to a community of like-minded professionals. Attend meetings, conferences, and networking events organized by these groups to connect with industry peers, access resources, and stay updated on industry trends, reinforcing your sense of belonging.

- **Initiate Conversations:** Be proactive in initiating conversations and introducing yourself to new people at networking events. Approach individuals with a friendly demeanor, ask open-ended questions, and show genuine interest in learning about their background, experiences, and interests.

- **Follow-Up:** After meeting new contacts, follow up with personalized emails, LinkedIn messages, or handwritten notes to express your appreciation for connecting and to continue the conversation. Offer to meet for coffee, schedule a follow-up call, or invite them to future networking events to nurture the relationship further.

+ **Provide Value:** Look for opportunities to provide value to your network by sharing relevant articles, offering assistance or resources, or making introductions to other professionals. Demonstrating your willingness to help and contribute to others' success strengthens your relationships and fosters reciprocity.

+ **Maintain Relationships:** Stay in touch with your network regularly by sending updates, sharing relevant information, or scheduling catch-up meetings. Building and maintaining strong relationships requires ongoing communication and engagement to keep connections active and meaningful.

+ **Offer Help:** Be generous with your time, expertise, and resources through helping, mentorship, or supporting others in your network. Assisting others strengthens your relationships and establishes you as a valuable and reliable professional community member.

+ **Seek Diverse Connections:** Expand your network by connecting with individuals from diverse backgrounds, industries, and perspectives. Building a diverse network enriches your professional experience, exposes you to new ideas, and opens doors to unexpected opportunities.

+ **Give First:** Offering value, support, or resources to others builds trust and strengthens relationships. This principle encourages a mindset of generosity and collaboration rather than transactional interactions.

+ **Build Authentic Relationships:** Authenticity is crucial in networking. It helps build genuine connections based on mutual interests and shared values. Authentic relationships are more likely to be lasting and meaningful than superficial or purely professional.

+ **Create a Personal Network Map:** Create a 'network map' to keep track of your connections and understand how they relate to your goals. This tool helps you identify key people and strategize how to maintain and leverage these relationships.

- **Invest in Relationships:** Networking requires ongoing effort. Regularly engage with your network through follow-ups, check-ins, and personalized communication. Investing time and effort into relationships helps maintain strong connections and keeps you at the top of your mind.

- **Be a Connector:** Become a connector by introducing people who might benefit from knowing each other. This act of connecting others not only adds value but also positions you as a valuable network resource.

- **Cultivate a Network of Diverse Contacts:** A diverse network can provide broader insights, opportunities, and support. Seek out and build relationships with people from different industries, backgrounds, and areas of expertise.

- **Leverage Networking Opportunities:** Actively seek and leverage networking opportunities, such as industry events, social gatherings, and professional groups. Being proactive and visible in these settings can help expand your network and open up new possibilities.

- **Follow Up and Stay Engaged:** Follow up with new contacts and stay engaged over time. Ferrazzi stresses keeping relationships warm through regular communication and meaningful interactions.

Reid Hoffman's genius lies in his ability to see connections where others see isolation. He didn't just create a platform through LinkedIn; he revolutionized how professionals build networks, exchange value, and unlock opportunities.

Reid Hoffman, Co-Founder of LinkedIn on Developing Professional Networks

Reid Hoffman is a highly influential entrepreneur, venture capitalist, and author, best known as the co-founder of LinkedIn. His background is diverse, combining a solid academic foundation with extensive experience in the tech industry and venture capital. Reid Hoffman, a prominent entrepreneur and investor, has shared valuable insights on developing and leveraging professional networks.

Reid Hoffman's networking story is a testament to the idea that success is often built on the relationships you cultivate. His career demonstrates how strategic and authentic networking can lead to incredible opportunities and long-term success.

Key Networking Lessons from Reid Hoffman:

+ **Start Early:** Build your network as early as possible and continue nurturing it throughout your career.

+ **Value Authentic Relationships:** Focus on developing genuine connections rather than expanding your contact list.

+ **Leverage Networks for Mutual Benefit:** Use your network to create win-win situations where both parties benefit.

+ **Be a Connector:** Help others by introducing them to people who can help them, strengthening your network.

+ **Continuously Engage:** Regularly maintain and refresh your network relationships through consistent communication and support.

Barriers to SMART Networking

Overcoming barriers in networking is like breaking through walls of isolation, forging connections that bridge divides, and paving the way to boundless opportunities and meaningful relationships.

Barriers That Hinder Effective Networking:

+ **Time Constraints:** Busy schedules and competing priorities can make allocating time for networking activities challenging. Balancing work, family commitments, and personal responsibilities may limit the ability to attend networking events or engage in networking activities regularly.

+ **Lack of Confidence:** We may feel apprehensive or insecure about networking, particularly in unfamiliar or intimidating social settings. A lack of confidence in our communication skills, social interactions, or ability to make meaningful connections can hinder us from actively participating in networking opportunities.

+ **Fear of Rejection:** Fear of rejection or social anxiety may prevent us from initiating conversations, introducing ourselves to new people, or reaching out to potential contacts. The fear of being perceived as intrusive or facing rejection can inhibit us from proactively expanding our network and building relationships.

+ **Limited Network Resources:** We may face barriers to networking due to limited access to networking resources or opportunities. Geographic location, industry-specific networking events, or lack of connections within certain professional circles can restrict our ability to expand our network and access valuable networking opportunities.

+ **Lack of Networking Skills:** Inadequate networking skills, including communication, interpersonal, and relationship-building skills, can hinder effectiveness in networking. Difficulty initiating conversations, maintaining engaging interactions, or following up with contacts can limit the ability to build and sustain meaningful relationships through networking.

+ **Social and Cultural Barriers:** Social and cultural factors, such as language, cultural differences, or social norms, can create barriers to effective networking, particularly in diverse or multicultural settings. Differences in communication styles, networking etiquette, and cultural expectations may impact your ability to connect and build relationships across different social and cultural contexts.

+ **Networking Burnout:** Overwhelming networking demands, constant social interactions, or excessive networking activities can lead to burnout. We may experience fatigue, disengagement, or a lack of enthusiasm for networking, leading to decreased motivation and effectiveness in building and maintaining relationships.

Addressing these barriers requires us to develop strategies to overcome obstacles, such as prioritizing networking activities, building confidence through practice and preparation, seeking support and guidance from mentors or networking groups, and continuously improving networking skills through learning and development initiatives. Additionally, creating inclusive and accessible networking environments that accommodate diverse backgrounds, preferences, and needs can help reduce barriers and facilitate effective networking for everyone.

> "You can make more friends in two months by becoming genuinely interested in other people than you can in two years by trying to get other people interested in you."
> –Dale Carnegie—*How to Win Friends and Influence People*

Social Capital—Networking Benefit

Social capital refers to the collective value that arises from social networks.

relationships, and connections within a community or society. This includes the resources, benefits, and advantages you or groups can gain through social interactions and networks. In other words, social capital is the influence of being part of a community or society and having strong connections with others. It can be a powerful asset in many areas of life, such as business, politics, and personal relationships.

Critical Aspects of Social Capital:

Networks and Relationships: The foundation of social capital lies in the relationships and connections between people, groups, organizations, and communities. This includes strong bonds, such as close relationships with family, friends, and colleagues, and weaker connections with acquaintances and diverse groups.

- **Trust and Reciprocity:** Trust and reciprocity are crucial for developing social capital. Trust forms the basis of cooperative and dependable actions among individuals, while reciprocity involves exchanging resources, support, and favors within social networks. Both trust and reciprocity play a significant role in building social capital, providing a foundation for cooperative and reliable actions within social networks.

- **Information and Knowledge Sharing:** Exchanging ideas, experiences, and expertise drives innovation, learning, and problem-solving. Social capital plays a critical role in facilitating the flow of information and knowledge, enabling the exchange of resources and opportunities. Trust and reciprocity are indispensable components in constructing social capital, providing a basis for cooperative and reliable actions within social networks.

- **Social Norms and Cohesion:** Creating shared values, norms, and social cohesion is crucial for promoting cooperation, collaboration, and a sense of belonging within a community or group. Social capital plays an indispensable role in developing these shared norms and collective identities, which helps to strengthen the sense of togetherness and cooperation among members.

+ **Social Support and Influence**: Access to social support networks can be crucial for individuals needing emotional, instrumental, or informational assistance. Social capital can access and influence an individual's behavior, attitudes, and decision-making through social norms, role models, and social pressure.

You can create and maintain social capital by dedicating time and effort to building trust, nurturing relationships, attending community events, and engaging in social networks. This way, you, as well as other people and communities, can harness the power of social connections to promote positive change and enjoy mutual benefits. Let us actively cultivate our social capital to unlock our full potential and achieve great things together!

Developing Role Models—Networking Benefit

Positive role models are essential for personal growth, well-being, and a sense of purpose. It is important to recognize that role models can come from various areas of life, including family, friends, community leaders, historical figures, and professionals. Role models inspire us to emulate their behavior, actions, and achievements.

Positive Role Model Benefits:

+ **Inspiration:** Role models can motivate and encourage you to set and pursue your goals and aspirations.

+ **Guidance:** Role models can guide and advise you on achieving success and navigating challenges based on their experiences and expertise.

- **Self-esteem:** Seeing someone embodying qualities and values can boost self-esteem and self-confidence.

- **Personal Development:** Role models can encourage personal growth and development by serving as examples of overcoming obstacles, developing skills, and achieving success.

- **Values and Morals:** Role models can positively influence values and morals, as you may see examples of ethical behavior and integrity.

- **Community Engagement:** Role models inspire you to engage with their communities and make a positive impact, serving as examples of giving back and making a difference.

Having positive role models can help you develop positive traits and behaviors that contribute to personal and professional success and the betterment of society.

Steps to Develop Role Models:

- **Identify Your Values:** Reflect on the qualities and characteristics that you admire in others. Consider the values important to you and the person you aspire to be.

- **Seek Inspiration:** Look for individuals who embody the values and traits you admire. These can be people you know personally, public figures, historical figures, or fictional characters.

- **Study Their Behavior:** Observe how your role models behave in various situations. Please pay attention to their actions, decisions, and interactions with others. Note what you find inspiring or admirable about their behavior.

- **Learn From Their Experiences:** Study your role models' life stories and experiences. Understand the challenges they faced, the obstacles they overcame, and the lessons they learned along the way.

* **Emulate Positive Qualities:** Identify specific qualities or behaviors exhibited by your role models that you would like to cultivate in yourself. Make a conscious effort to incorporate these qualities into your life and actions.

* **Set Goals:** Use your role models to inspire you to set meaningful goals. Break down your goals into actionable steps and work towards them with determination and perseverance.

* **Be Open to Growth:** Recognize that nobody is perfect. When it comes to your role models, allow yourself to learn and grow from both their successes and their failures. Use their example as motivation to strive for self-improvement continuously.

* **Be a Role Model Yourself:** As you develop and grow, strive to become a positive influence and role model for others. Lead by example and demonstrate the values and qualities that you admire in your role models.

By following these steps and remaining committed to personal growth and development, you can cultivate your role models and become the best version of yourself.

My Story—Role Model

By harnessing the power of networking, I linked my team to the best-selling marketing and sales book on Amazon. This decision proved to be a game-changer. By applying the SMART networking strategies and leveraging our network, my team achieved an impressive daily billing of $10,000, demonstrating the undeniable impact of effective networking and the right resources in driving exceptional business outcomes. Through strategic use of LinkedIn and tapping into my connections, we obtained valuable insights and strategies that directly contributed to our success.

This event taught us that professional networking can lead to impressive results when done in the best interests of the established connections.

Networking Benefits:

- ✦ Combining resources increased the size of the project and its success.
- ✦ We were able to ramp up a team quickly.
- ✦ We have improved our ability to offer an effective solution that addresses the client's needs.
- ✦ Provided guidance and expertise.

In summary, networking and developing connections can be superpowers and skills that can lead to personal and professional success.

Networking opens doors to opportunities, fosters collaboration, and builds relationships that can elevate your personal and professional growth. It's not just about who you know, but how you connect and create value together.

Summary

Networking provides numerous benefits that contribute to personal and professional growth. By expanding one's circle of contacts and developing meaningful relationships, networking offers access to new opportunities, such as career advancements, business partnerships, and personal development. Through knowledge sharing and collaboration, you gain valuable insights, stay informed about industry trends, and enhance your skills. Networking also facilitates resource access, providing mentorship, advice, and support from experienced professionals. Moreover, networking is critical in career advancement as you build visibility, credibility, and professional connections within your industry. Additionally, networking promotes personal development by boosting self-confidence, communication skills, and interpersonal relationships. Overall, networking empowers you to navigate your professional journey with confidence, resilience, and a sense of community, leading to personal and professional success.

Building a network is more than just collecting contacts; it is about nurturing meaningful connections, where each interaction is an opportunity to gain experience, grow, and collaborate. In the realm of smart networking, success is not measured by the size of your network but by the depth of your relationships and the value you bring to each connection.

Action Plan

Develop SMART Networking Goals:

1. Write down the SMART goals for developing connections and relationships.

2. Identify and connect with people and organizations to contact.

3. Develop and write down the techniques and strategies for initiating contact with and connecting with others to achieve your goals.

4. Understand the benefits relationships you bring to the connection and relationship.

5. Develop trust-based relationship values and virtues you bring to the relationship.

CHAPTER 11

Dealing With Toxic People

"Keep away from people who try to belittle your ambitions."

Mark Twain—Author

Dealing with Toxic People and Behavior

In this exploration, we delve into the intricate dynamics of human interactions and offer insights into recognizing and effectively addressing toxic behavior. Understanding toxic relationships' underlying patterns, motivations, and impact empowers us to navigate these challenges with clarity, resilience, and grace. This guide will teach you to transform challenges into opportunities for personal growth, empowerment, and a more harmonious life.

Recognizing toxic behavior is the first step toward maintaining healthy relationships and protecting one's well-being. When dealing with toxic individuals, it is vital to set boundaries, communicate assertively, and consider seeking support from friends, family, or professionals.

Dealing with toxic people can feel isolating and overwhelming, but it's important to remember that you are not alone. Many have faced similar challenges and emerged stronger by seeking support, setting boundaries, and prioritizing their well-being. Whether through friends, family, or professional help, reaching out can provide the strength and perspective to navigate toxic situations. Sharing your experiences can also help you realize that others understand your struggles and that together, you can find ways to protect your peace and reclaim your happiness. You don't have to face toxicity alone—a community is ready to support you.

"When someone shows you who they are, believe them the first time."

Maya Angelou—Poet

Types of Toxic People and Behavior

Have you ever felt unsafe, unsettled, and unsure in a work or personal environment? You may be around toxic people and toxic leaders. The following people may describe some of the characters and personalities around you.

Seven Types of Toxic Individuals Characterized by Specific Traits and Patterns of Behavior:

+ **The Criticizer:** The Criticizer constantly finds fault, criticizes, and belittles others, creating a demoralizing atmosphere that undermines confidence and self-esteem. This toxic environment can reduce morale, productivity, and team trust.

- **The Manipulator:** A manipulative individual uses deceit and guilt-tripping to control others, exploiting vulnerabilities and undermining trust. This erodes relationships, damages cohesion, and fosters a toxic atmosphere that hinders communication and collaboration.

- **The Victim:** Someone who habitually plays the victim and avoids responsibility can be emotionally draining. This behavior saps others' emotional energy and hinders progress and collaboration.

- **The Energy Vampire:** Constantly negative people who frequently complain can emotionally drain others, leading to exhaustion among colleagues. This behavior hinders positive interactions, stifles creativity, and reduces productivity.

- **The Narcissist:** A self-centered individual lacking empathy seeks constant admiration and often manipulates others for personal gain. Their behavior prioritizes self-interest over others, undermining trust, eroding team cohesion, and fostering resentment, ultimately harming well-being and collective goals.

- **The Gossiper:** An individual who spreads rumors, gossips, and thrives on drama can disrupt a group or organization. Their behavior undermines trust, creates a toxic environment, and damages relationships and team morale, challenging maintaining a healthy, collaborative atmosphere.

- **The Control Freak:** An excessively controlling and possessive individual can limit the personal freedom of others, stifle creativity, and create tension and resentment. Over time, this behavior can harm relationships, morale, and collective progress.

It is essential to recognize these toxic behaviors and establish boundaries to protect your well-being. Dealing with toxic individuals may involve setting clear limits, practicing self-care, and, in some cases, distancing yourself from those who consistently exhibit harmful behaviors.

Toxic Behavior Described

Toxic behavior refers to actions, attitudes, and patterns of interaction that hurt others or oneself. It can be emotionally draining while damaging relationships and hindering personal growth.

Toxic Behavior Examples:

+ **Manipulation**: Manipulative individuals use tactics to control and influence others for their gain, often by playing on emotions, guilt, or insecurities.

+ **Constant Criticism**: People who consistently criticize, belittle, or undermine others can create an environment of negativity and low self-esteem.

+ **Gaslighting**: Gaslighting involves distorting facts or reality to make others doubt their perceptions, feelings, and memories, causing confusion and self-doubt.

+ **Passive-Aggressiveness**: Passive-aggressive behavior involves indirect expressions of hostility or dissatisfaction, often through sarcasm, avoidance, or subtle digs.

+ **Jealousy and Envy**: Individuals who exhibit intense jealousy or envy can foster a toxic atmosphere of competition, resentment, and insecurity.

+ **Blaming and Deflecting Responsibility**: People who refuse to take responsibility for their actions and consistently shift blame onto others can create a culture of distrust.

+ **Negativity and Pessimism**: Constant negativity and pessimism can drain the energy of those around them and hinder constructive problem-solving.

- **Entitlement**: Entitled individuals believe they deserve special treatment or privileges, leading to disrespect and disregarding others and their needs.

- **Drama Creation**: Those who thrive on creating or exacerbating conflicts and drama can disrupt relationships and destabilize harmony.

- **Isolation and Control**: Individuals who isolate others from their friends, family, or support systems and exert control over their lives can create unhealthy dependence.

- **Passive Behavior**: Passive behavior involves consistently avoiding conflicts or confrontation, which can lead to unresolved issues and unexpressed feelings.

- **Disrespect**: Disrespectful behavior, such as mocking, insulting, or belittling others, erodes trust and dignity in relationships.

- **Boundary Violation**: Individuals who disregard personal boundaries, invade privacy, and overstep limits can create discomfort and stress.

- **Gossip and Backbiting**: Spreading rumors, gossiping, and engaging in negative discussions about others can damage reputations and foster mistrust.

- **Explosive Anger**: People with intense and unpredictable outbursts of anger can create an environment of fear and instability.

Recognizing toxic behavior is the first step toward maintaining healthy relationships and protecting one's well-being. When dealing with toxic individuals, it is essential to set boundaries, communicate assertively, and consider seeking support from friends, family, or professionals.

Dealing with toxic people and behavior requires a proactive and mindful approach to safeguard one's well-being while maintaining healthy boundaries. It involves recognizing the signs of toxicity, such as manipulation, negativity, and emotional abuse, and taking steps to protect oneself from their harmful effects. These steps may include setting clear boundaries, practicing assertive communication, and prioritizing self-care.

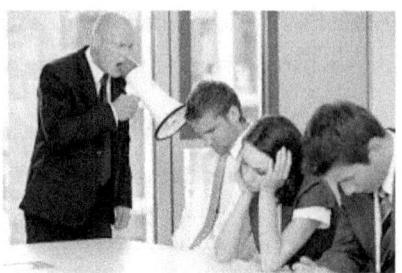

Toxic People and Your Self-Esteem

Toxic individuals can significantly affect our self-esteem through their negative behaviors, criticisms, and manipulations. Over time, their actions can erode our confidence and self-worth.

Ways Toxic People Can Harm Your Self-esteem:

1. **Constant Criticism:** Toxic people relentlessly criticize others, pointing out their flaws and shortcomings. This can make us doubt our abilities and values.

2. **Manipulation:** Toxic people may manipulate us to serve their needs or agendas, leaving you powerless and questioning your judgment.

3. **Gaslighting:** A form of manipulation where the toxic person denies our reality, making you doubt your perceptions and memories. This can lead to confusion and a loss of trust in yourself.

4. **Undermining Confidence:** Toxic individuals may belittle our achievements or goals, making you feel like you are not good enough or capable of success.

5. **Emotional Abuse:** This can include insults, threats, or guilt-tripping, deeply impacting our self-esteem and making us feel unworthy of love and respect.

6. **Isolation:** Toxic people may try to isolate us from supportive friends and family members, leaving us with fewer sources of positive reinforcement and validation.

7. **Comparison:** Toxic individuals may constantly compare us to others in a negative light, making us feel inadequate or inferior.

8. **Boundary Violations:** Toxic people often disregard our boundaries and personal space, leaving us feeling disrespected and devalued.

Dealing with toxic people can be challenging, but it is essential to prioritize our well-being. Setting boundaries, seeking support from trusted friends or a therapist, and practicing self-care are crucial steps in protecting our self-esteem from the adverse effects of toxic relationships. You deserve to be treated with kindness, respect, and understanding. It is essential always to remember that!

"When you don't confront the bad behavior of toxic people, you're inadvertently encouraging it. Stand up to toxicity, set clear boundaries, and surround yourself with positivity."

Bob Sutton—Author—*Good Boss, Bad Boss*

Solutions to Toxic People and Behavior

Dealing with toxic people can be challenging, but it is essential to prioritize your well-being and mental health. In his book *Good Boss, Bad Boss*, Bob Sutton provides valuable insights on dealing with toxic people in the workplace. He emphasizes the importance of setting clear boundaries and not allowing toxic individuals to dominate or drain your energy. Sutton advises maintaining a distance from such people, both physically and emotionally, to protect your well-being. He also stresses the need to cultivate a strong support network of positive and trustworthy colleagues who can offer advice and solidarity. When confrontation is necessary, Sutton suggests being firm and clear about unacceptable behaviors while remaining calm and professional.

Ultimately, his approach underscores the importance of preserving mental and emotional health, prioritizing constructive relationships, and creating a work environment where toxic behavior is unacceptable.

Checklist to Help You Stay Away from Toxic Individuals:

+ **Set Boundaries:** Establish clear boundaries and communicate them assertively. Tell toxic people what behavior is unacceptable; consequences may follow if they cross those boundaries.

+ **Recognize Manipulation:** Avoid manipulation tactics, such as guilt-tripping, gaslighting, and victim playing. Toxic individuals often use these tactics to control and manipulate others.

+ **Trust Your Instincts:** Listen to your gut feelings. If someone consistently makes you feel uncomfortable, drained, or anxious, it is a sign that they might be toxic.

+ **Limit Interaction:** Gradually reduce the amount of time you spend with toxic individuals. This can help you disengage from their negative influence.

+ **Surround Yourself with Positivity:** Find relationships with people who uplift and support you. Surrounding yourself with positivity can counteract the effects of toxic interactions.

+ **Practice Self-Care:** Prioritize self-care activities that nourish your mental and emotional well-being. Engage in hobbies, exercise, meditation, and spending time with loved ones.

+ **Seek Support:** Confide with friends, family members, or a therapist about your experiences. They can provide perspective, guidance, and emotional support.

+ **Stay Objective:** When interacting with toxic individuals, maintain objectivity. Do not take their negativity personally and avoid getting entangled in their drama.

- **Learn to Say No:** Be confident about requests or uncomfortable situations. Toxic individuals often exploit people's inability to set boundaries.

- **Avoid Justifying:** You do not need to justify your decision to distance yourself from toxic people. Your well-being is a valid reason.

- **Focus on Solutions:** Instead of dwelling on a situation's toxicity, focus on finding solutions or strategies to minimize its impact on you.

- **Practice Empathy from a Distance:** While you should prioritize your well-being, practicing empathy from a distance can help you understand the underlying reasons for someone's toxic behavior without getting emotionally involved.

- **Build a Support Network:** Surround yourself with supportive friends, family, and colleagues who can provide encouragement and advice.

- **Educate Yourself:** Read books, articles, or attend workshops about dealing with toxic people and setting healthy boundaries.

- **Practice Detachment:** Emotionally detach yourself from the toxic behavior. Remember that you cannot control their actions but can manage your reactions.

- **Forgive for Your Peace:** Forgiveness does not mean condoning toxic behavior. It is about freeing yourself from the burden of holding onto anger or resentment.

Dealing with toxic people involves a threefold approach: identifying, recognizing their behaviors, and implementing practical solutions. It is essential to prioritize one's well-being and mental health, realizing that distancing oneself from toxic influences can be a crucial step toward personal growth and a healthier, more positive environment. Remember, prioritizing your well-being and mental health is paramount.

Even Taylor Swift, at the height of her success, had to navigate the challenges of toxic people. Her journey reminds us that setting boundaries and staying true to ourselves is key to rising above negativity and thriving.

Taylor Swift—Dealing with Toxicity

In 2019, Taylor Swift made headlines when she publicly spoke out about her struggle with her former record label, Big Machine Records, and its founder, Scott Borchetta. The conflict arose when Swift discovered that the masters of her first six albums were sold to music executive Scooter Braun without her knowledge or consent. Swift described the experience as deeply hurtful, especially given her long-standing grievances with Braun, whom she accused of bullying and toxic behavior in the past.

Dealing with Toxicity

+ **Speaking Out**: Swift spoke publicly about her experiences instead of staying silent. She took to social media to share her side of the story, shedding light on the power dynamics and toxic practices within the music industry. By doing so, she advocated for herself and brought attention to broader issues many artists face.

+ **Taking Control of Her Work**: Rather than being defeated by the situation, Swift took control of her music career by re-recording her old albums. This move allowed her to regain ownership of her work and continue sharing her music with fans on her terms. It was a powerful statement against the toxic practices of those who sought to control her art.

+ **Maintaining Integrity**: Throughout the ordeal, Swift remained true to her values and maintained her integrity. She refused to back down or compromise, even when faced with significant challenges from powerful industry figures. This perseverance earned her respect and admiration from her fans and peers alike.

+ **Focusing on Positive Relationships**: Despite the negativity surrounding the situation, Swift continued to focus on her positive relationships, both personal and professional. She surrounded herself with supportive friends, collaborators, and fans who uplifted her during a difficult time.

+ **Outcome:** Taylor Swift's handling of this situation is an inspiring example of dealing with toxic people and environments. By speaking out, taking control of her work, and maintaining her integrity, she turned a challenging situation into an opportunity for growth and empowerment. Her story resonates with many who have faced similar struggles and highlights the importance of standing up for oneself in toxicity.

Even amidst the presence of toxic people, the key to thriving lies in building an unshakable core of self-worth. Let their negativity be your reminder to grow stronger and shine brighter.

My Story of Dealing with Toxic People

In my personal development journey, I took a coaching course to enhance my skills and gain valuable insights into effective leadership and mentorship. Initially, the conversations with my coach were positive and encouraging, offering constructive feedback and fostering an environment of growth. However, as time passed, I noticed a shift in her approach. Her comments, which had once been supportive, became increasingly hostile.

This change was disheartening, especially as her criticisms were directed at me and made publicly, which compounded the impact. To make matters worse, she involved her colleagues and director, who continued the trend of negative commentary. This collective shift in attitude created a challenging and uncomfortable environment, making it difficult to maintain the positive and productive coaching experience I had initially anticipated.

My stress levels became maxed out. I was emotionally and psychologically highly stressed. To survive the environment, I confronted her, and she denied any accountability or responsibility for her behavior.

I finished the coaching course, stressed and disappointed. This course had become a train wreck, and I was frustrated with it initially.

At the end of the course, while it was frustrating to be personally attacked by a toxic personality, I decided to use this as a learning experience. The following are the actions I took:

1. I began to study the impact of toxic people professionally and personally. This decision made me less of a victim, and now I have become a researcher. I could educate people on the impact of toxic people. The chapter in this book is one example.

2. I discovered the types of toxic people and their behavior types. I could now identify the behaviors that toxic people exhibit.

3. I studied the solutions, tools, and tactics we can use when dealing with toxic people.

4. I learned that I am not alone when dealing with toxic people and their environments.

5. I am now more aware and have increased my ability to avoid toxicity because of my self-awareness.

Learning to overcome dealing with toxic people builds emotional resilience, sharpens our boundaries, and frees our energy for meaningful relationships. It empowers you to protect your well-being while focusing on your goals and values.

Summary

Dealing with toxic people requires a combination of setting boundaries, maintaining emotional distance, and fostering a positive support network. Establishing clear limits on what behavior we tolerate and communicating those boundaries assertively is essential. Limit interactions with toxic individuals to minimize their impact on your well-being. Cultivating relationships with supportive, positive people can help counterbalance the negativity and provide strength during challenging situations. Additionally, practicing self-care and focusing on what you can control maintains your mental and emotional health. When confrontation is necessary, approach it calmly, addressing the behavior rather than engaging in conflict. By implementing these strategies, you can protect yourself and maintain a healthy, productive environment despite toxic individuals.

Cultivating a supportive network of positive relationships can buffer against toxic influences, offering validation and support. Recognizing and addressing toxic behavior assertively and compassionately can create a healthier and more positive environment for yourself and those around you.

Toxic people are like dark clouds; they may try to overshadow your light but cannot extinguish it if you do not let them. So be sure to protect your energy and surround yourself with positivity.

Action Plan

Reminder: toxic people can impact our lives in several ways—financially, physically, and psychologically.

1. Write down the toxic people that may impact your life.

2. Write down these people's toxic and negative impact on your life.

3. Review the techniques and tools available to counteract toxic people's impact on your life.

4. Develop an action plan and strategy to outmaneuver and outthink toxic people.

5. Ask for feedback and support from trusted relationships to review your thinking and strategies regarding toxic people.

CHAPTER 12

Putting It All Together: Self-Leadership, Self-Discovery, and Self-Empowerment

"Any time you have an opportunity to make a difference in this world, and you don't, then you are wasting your time on Earth."

Roberto Clemente—Hall of Fame Baseball Player and Humanitarian

Congratulations! Putting It All Together

Congratulations on embarking on this exhilarating journey where every challenge pushes you to exceed your limits, and every setback inspires you to delve deeper within yourself. As the hero of this story, you begin with uncertainty but a burning desire to make a meaningful impact. Along the way, you face obstacles that demand more than skill—they require unwavering courage, unshakeable faith, and a steadfast commitment to your values. Courage is honed as you confront your fears head-on, recognizing that true bravery lies in taking action despite fear. Faith flourishes as you embrace the process, trusting that every arduous step guides you toward your ultimate destination. Your values serve as your guiding star, navigating you through the most challenging decisions ,and enabling you to remain authentic to yourself. Through this journey, you emerge as a survivor and a triumphant leader, having carved a path through adversity with resolute integrity, unyielding strength, and an unwavering belief in the power of perseverance.

Combining self-leadership and self-discovery is vital for personal and professional growth. Self-leadership means taking responsibility for your actions, setting clear goals, and motivating yourself to achieve them. It involves understanding your strengths and weaknesses, iden-tified through a SWOT analysis. Self-discovery complements this by fostering awareness of your values, passions, and aspirations. When you combine self-leadership and self-discovery, you create a roadmap for continuous improvement and resilience. This synergy enables you to navigate challenges confidently, leverage growth opportunities, and lead a fulfilling and purposeful life. Embracing this integrated approach ensures that you are not just reacting to circumstances but actively shaping your journey and making informed, strategic decisions that align with your true self.

Embracing self-leadership empowers you to take control of your life by making decisions that align with your values and goals. By actively guiding your path, you cultivate confidence, knowing that you can navigate challenges and pursue your aspirations. This control fosters resilience, allowing you to bounce back from setbacks with a stronger, more determined mindset. Additionally, self-leadership enhances self-awareness as you become more attuned to your strengths, weaknesses, and motivations. This awareness not only helps you make better choices but also allows you to grow continuously, evolving into the best version of yourself.

"The first and best victory is to conquer yourself."

Plato—Greek Philosopher

The Power of Self-Leadership Benefits

Self-leadership intentionally influences your thinking, behavior, and actions to achieve your objectives. It involves taking responsibility for your personal and professional growth and offers numerous benefits that can enhance various aspects of your life. Here are some key benefits of self-leadership:

+ **Increased Self-Awareness:** Self-leadership helps you better understand your strengths, weaknesses, values, and motivations. This self-awareness is crucial for making informed decisions and aligning your actions with your personal and professional goals.

+ **Greater Accountability:** By practicing self-leadership, you take ownership of your actions and their outcomes. This accountability fosters a sense of responsibility and encourages you to stay committed to your goals, leading to higher personal and professional achievement.

+ **Enhanced Motivation and Discipline:** Self-leaders are typically more motivated because they set goals and create pathways to success. They also develop the discipline to stay focused and persevere through challenges, essential for long-term success.

+ **Improved Decision-Making:** With self-leadership, you become more adept at making decisions aligned with your values and objectives. You learn to trust your judgment, weigh options carefully, and choose actions that move you closer to your goals.

+ **Better Time Management and Productivity:** Self-leadership involves setting clear priorities and managing time effectively. By taking control of your schedule and focusing on what matters most, you can boost your productivity and achieve more in less time.

+ **Resilience and Adaptability:** Self-leaders are better equipped to handle setbacks and adapt to change. By taking control of their reactions and maintaining a positive mindset, they can navigate challenges with resilience and become stronger on the other side.

+ **Greater Career Success:** In the workplace, self-leadership can lead to faster career progression. Employers value individuals who can manage themselves effectively, set and achieve goals, and contribute positively to the organization without constant supervision.

+ **Improved Relationships:** Self-leadership encourages you to communicate effectively, manage conflicts, and build healthy personal and professional relationships. By understanding and leading yourself, you can interact with others more empathetically and constructively.

+ **Increased Confidence:** Your confidence naturally increases as you take control of your life and progress toward your goals. This self-assurance empowers you to take on new challenges and seize opportunities you previously hesitated to pursue.

+ **Personal Fulfillment and Happiness:** Self-leadership enables you to live a life aligned with your values and aspirations. By taking charge of your own growth and direction, you can create a meaningful and fulfilling life, leading to greater overall happiness.

+ **Continuous Growth and Development:** Self-leaders are committed to lifelong learning and personal development. They seek opportunities to grow through new experiences, education, or self-reflection and continuously strive to improve themselves.

- **Empowerment and Independence:** Self-leadership empowers you to take control of your life, making you less reliant on others for direction and motivation. This independence fosters a sense of autonomy and freedom, allowing you to chart your own course.

In summary, self-leadership is a powerful tool for personal and professional success. By leading yourself effectively, you can achieve your goals, build strong relationships, and live a more fulfilling and purposeful life.

"You have power over your mind—not outside events. Realize this, and you will find strength."

Marcus Aurelius—Stoic Philosopher

Self-Empowerment

Self-empowerment leads to greater control over your life, increased self-esteem, and a stronger sense of purpose. It enables you to take proactive steps towards achieving your goals and living a fulfilling life.

Self-empowerment is taking control of your life and making informed, confident decisions. It involves recognizing and utilizing your strengths, skills, and abilities to take charge of your personal and professional life.

Essential Aspects of Self-Empowerment

1. **Self-Awareness:** Understanding your needs, desires, values, and goals. This self-knowledge provides a foundation for making choices that align with your true self.

2. **Confidence:** Build self-confidence and believe in your ability to effect change and overcome challenges. This includes trusting your judgment and skills.

3. **Autonomy:** Taking responsibility for your actions and decisions and recognizing that you can influence your own outcomes. It involves making choices that align with your values and goals rather than relying on others to define your path.

4. **Skill Development:** Continuously improving your skills and competencies to enhance your ability to tackle challenges and seize opportunities. This includes seeking out learning opportunities and being open to growth.

5. **Resilience:** Developing the ability to bounce back from setbacks and view challenges as opportunities for growth. Resilience involves maintaining a positive outlook and persistence in the face of adversity.

6. **Assertiveness:** Clearly and confidently expressing your needs, desires, and boundaries while respecting others. Assertiveness helps you advocate for yourself and create healthy relationships.

7. **Decision-Making:** Making informed and deliberate choices based on your values and goals rather than being swayed by external pressures or opinions.

Self-empowerment results in greater control over your life, increased self-esteem, and a stronger sense of purpose. It allows you to take proactive steps toward achieving your goals and living a fulfilling life.

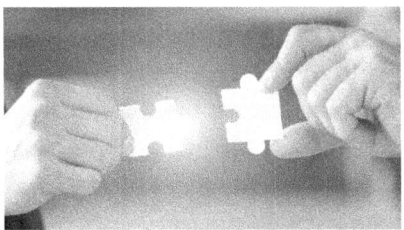

The Interconnection of Self-Leadership and Self-Discovery

Self-leadership and self-discovery are interconnected processes that, when combined, create a robust framework for personal and professional growth. Understanding and leading oneself enables you to unlock your full potential, achieve meaningful goals, and lead fulfilling lives.

+ **Enhanced Self-Awareness:** Self-discovery involves exploring one's values, strengths, weaknesses, passions, and aspirations. This deep understanding of oneself is essential for effective self-leadership. Knowing who and what you want enables you to lead yourself with clarity and purpose.

+ **Improved Motivation and Goal Setting:** Through self-discovery, you identify your intrinsic motivations and set goals that align with your values and passions. Self-leadership involves creating actionable plans to achieve these goals and maintaining motivation through self-regulation and discipline.

+ **Greater Resilience and Adaptability:** Self-discovery helps you understand their responses to stress and adversity. With this knowledge, you can develop self-leadership strategies to enhance resilience, enabling you to bounce back from setbacks and adapt to changing circumstances.

+ **Personal Accountability and Integrity:** Understanding one's core values through self-discovery fosters a powerful sense of personal integrity. Self-leadership ensures that actions align with these values, promoting accountability and ethical behavior in personal and professional settings.

+ **Effective Time Management and Productivity:** Self-discovery involves recognizing how you work best, what distractions hinder you, and what environments are most conducive to your productivity. Self-leadership leverages this insight to implement effective time management strategies, enhancing productivity and work-life balance.

+ **Improved Interpersonal Relationships:** Through self-discovery, you gain insights into your communication styles, emotional triggers, and interpersonal dynamics. Self-leadership uses this understanding to cultivate better communication, empathy, and relationship-building skills.

+ **Continuous Learning and Growth:** Self-discovery is an ongoing process of learning about oneself. Self-leadership complements this by encouraging an initiative-taking approach to personal development, seeking growth opportunities, and embracing lifelong learning.

Self-leadership and self-discovery are deeply interconnected processes that, when unified, serve as a powerful framework for personal and professional growth. Embracing and guiding oneself empowers you to unlock your full potential, pursue meaningful goals, and live fulfilling lives.

Discovering Your Superpowers, Strengths, and Talents

Understanding your superpowers, strengths, and talents is a life-changing journey that helps you uncover the unique abilities you offer to the world. It all begins with self-awareness: taking a deep, honest look at what you excel at and are enthusiastic about. Reflect on your experiences, seek feedback from trusted peers, and engage in activities that challenge and excite you. As you pinpoint these inherent abilities, nurturing them through continuous learning and practice is essential. Surround yourself with mentors and supportive networks that promote growth and offer constructive feedback. Embrace opportunities that test your skills and take calculated risks that push you out of your comfort zone. This intentional effort enhances your strengths and builds confidence and resilience. By developing your superpowers, you can make a meaningful impact in your personal and professional life, opening doors to opportunities that align with your true potential and purpose.

Goal Setting—Tips and Techniques

Goal setting is a fundamental practice for achieving personal and professional success. It involves defining clear, specific, achievable objectives that provide direction and motivation. Effective goal setting begins with identifying what truly matters to you and aligning your goals with your values and long-term vision. Utilizing the SMART criteria—Specific, Measurable, Achievable, Relevant, and Time-bound—ensures your goals are well-structured and attainable. Additionally, breaking down larger goals into smaller, manageable tasks helps keep focus and momentum. Regularly reviewing and adjusting your goals allows for flexibility and continuous improvement. Setting and pursuing meaningful goals can enhance your focus, drive, and overall fulfillment in life.

"Live as if you were to die tomorrow. Learn as if you were to live forever."

Mahatma Gandhi

Learning—Your First Superpower

Learning as your first superpower is just the beginning of a lifelong journey of self-discovery and growth. As you continue to explore and develop your abilities, you will uncover new strengths and potentials, each adding to the tapestry of your unique talents. Embrace this journey with curiosity and enthusiasm, knowing that each step brings you closer to realizing your full potential and making a meaningful impact on the world.

SWOT Analysis—Your Strategic Tool

Conducting a personal SWOT analysis has benefits for your growth and development. You can better understand yourself by systematically examining your strengths, weaknesses, opportunities, and threats. This self-awareness can help you identify your unique talents and abilities, allowing you to leverage them in your personal and professional endeavors effectively. Recognizing weaknesses provides a roadmap for areas needing improvement, facilitating targeted skill development and personal growth. Opportunities highlight potential avenues for advancement and new experiences, encouraging initiative-taking pursuit of goals. Understanding threats enables you to anticipate and mitigate challenges, fostering resilience and strategic planning. A personal SWOT analysis empowers you to make informed decisions, maximize your potential, and navigate your life confidently and clearly.

Developing a Growth and Grit Mindset

Developing a growth and grit mindset offers transformative benefits that can significantly enhance personal and professional success. A growth mindset believes you can improve your abilities and intelligence through effort and learning, fostering resilience, curiosity, and a love of learning. This perspective encourages you to embrace challenges, learn from criticism, and persist in the face of setbacks, viewing them as opportunities for growth. Complementing this, grit—the combination of passion and perseverance for long-term goals—enables sustained effort and dedication. Together, these mindsets cultivate a robust inner drive and resilience, empowering you to overcome obstacles, achieve ambitious goals, and continuously improve. Embracing a growth and grit mindset enhances your ability to succeed and enriches your overall life experience, promoting continuous development and fulfillment.

Developing Mental Strength—Tools and Techniques

Developing a mental strength mindset involves cultivating resilience, perseverance, and a positive outlook in facing challenges and adversity. It begins with recognizing that setbacks and obstacles are part of life's journey and opportunities for growth. You can build resilience by reframing difficulties as learning experiences and opportunities to strengthen resolve. This mindset also involves practicing self-discipline and focusing on long-term goals, even in the face of short-term setbacks. Fostering a mental strength mindset requires cultivating a positive attitude, embracing change, and viewing failures as stepping stones toward success. Ultimately, developing mental strength empowers you to navigate life's uncertainties with confidence, adaptability, and an initiative-taking approach to personal and professional growth.

"Life is a journey, not a destination."

Ralph Waldo Emerson

Overcoming Procrastination

Conquering procrastination offers benefits that can enhance productivity, well-being, and overall success in personal and professional life. By overcoming procrastination, you gain control over your time and priorities, which leads to a sense of empowerment and accomplishment. This shift promotes greater efficiency and effectiveness in completing tasks, improving performance, and reducing stress. Overcoming procrastination also helps develop self-discipline, leading to consistent progress toward goals. Additionally, it improves decision-making skills by reducing the tendency to delay or avoid important choices. Embracing initiative-taking behaviors and breaking the cycle of procrastination increases productivity and boosts confidence, resilience, and overall satisfaction with life. Conquering procrastination empowers you to seize opportunities, achieve your aspirations, and lead more fulfilling lives.

Developing SMART Habits

Developing SMART (Specific, Measurable, Achievable, Relevant, Time-bound) habits offers transformative benefits that facilitate personal growth, productivity, and long-term success. These habits provide a structured framework for setting and achieving goals effectively. By being specific, you clarify intentions and focus efforts on tangible outcomes, enhancing clarity and direction in daily tasks. Measurable habits enable progress tracking, allowing you to monitor their advancement and make necessary adjustments. Achievable habits promote realistic goal attainment, fostering motivation and a sense of accomplishment. Moreover, relevant habits align with personal values and aspirations, ensuring actions are purpose-driven and meaningful. Time-bound habits establish deadlines, create urgency and accountability, encourage consistent effort, and prevent procrastination. Embracing SMART habits enhances productivity and cultivates discipline, resilience, and an initiative-taking mindset. These habits contribute to sustained personal development, enabling you to lead a fulfilling life and achieve your fullest potential.

SMART Networking for Personal and Professional Success

In today's interconnected world, SMART networking is critical for achieving personal and professional success. It goes beyond mere socializing to building relationships that create opportunities and drive growth strategically. SMART networking begins with clarity of purpose—understanding what you hope to achieve and how relationships can support those goals. It involves cultivating a genuine interest in others, listening actively, and offering mutual support and value. By leveraging platforms and events where like-minded individuals gather, you can expand your network strategically, connecting with mentors, collaborators, and potential clients or employers. Maintaining these connections through regular communication and thoughtful gestures reinforces trust and reciprocity. SMART networking also embraces diversity, recognizing the value of different perspectives and experiences in fostering innovation and learning. Ultimately, mastering the art of SMART networking enhances career prospects and enriches personal relationships, paving the way for lasting success and fulfillment in all aspects of life.

Dealing with Toxic People—Tools and Tactics

Dealing with toxic people can be emotionally draining and challenging, but employing tools and tactics can significantly mitigate their impact and promote healthier interactions. Firstly, having a repertoire of strategies allows you to set clear boundaries, which is crucial in protecting your well-being and maintaining your mental and emotional health. Tools such as assertive communication techniques help in expressing your needs and concerns effectively while minimizing conflict. Moreover, understanding and practicing emotional regulation techniques can prevent toxic interactions from escalating, allowing you to respond calmly and rationally in difficult situations.

Tactical approaches also include recognizing patterns of behavior and manipulation tactics used by toxic individuals. This awareness enables you to avoid being manipulated and make informed decisions about interacting or disengaging appropriately. Additionally, having support networks and seeking guidance from mentors or counselors provides validation and perspective, helping you navigate complex relationships more confidently. Ultimately, employing tools and tactics when dealing with toxic people empowers you to maintain control over your well-being, cultivate healthier relationships, and foster a more positive and constructive environment in both personal and professional settings.

"The secret of getting ahead is getting started."

Mark Twain—American Writer, Humorist, and Essayist

Action Steps—Where to Start

Embarking on the journey of self-discovery and leadership begins with fundamental steps:

1. **Self-Reflection:** Take the time to contemplate your values, passions, strengths, and weaknesses. Utilize journaling, meditation, and self-assessment tools for assistance.

2. **Set Clear Goals:** Identify what you aim to achieve personally and professionally. Setting specific, measurable, achievable, relevant, and time-bound (SMART) goals can provide guidance.

3. **Seek Feedback:** Request honest feedback from friends, family, colleagues, and mentors to gain valuable insights into your strengths and areas for improvement.

4. **Continuous Learning:** Commit to lifelong learning by reading books, taking courses, and attending workshops. Gaining new skills and knowledge enhances self-awareness and leadership abilities.

5. **Develop Self-Discipline:** Practice self-discipline by establishing routines, effectively managing your time, and staying focused on your goals.

6. **Act:** Begin by applying what you have learned about yourself in small steps. Experiment with different approaches, and do not be afraid to make mistakes, as they are part of the learning process.

7. **Build a Support Network:** Surround yourself with supportive and like-minded individuals who can provide encouragement, guidance, and accountability.

8. **Practice Mindfulness:** Engage in mindfulness practices such as meditation or yoga to stay present and connected with your inner self.

9. **Embrace Challenges:** Step out of your comfort zone and take on challenges that push your limits. This can lead to significant personal and professional growth.

10. **Reflect and Adjust:** Review your progress regularly and adjust as needed. Self-discovery and leadership development are ongoing processes that require flexibility and adaptability.

By following these steps, you can initiate a meaningful journey of self-discovery and leadership development, paving the way for personal growth and success.

"Self-leadership is the art of guiding yourself toward your highest potential. By mastering your thoughts, actions, and habits, you unlock the power to shape your life, overcome challenges, and inspire others through your example. The journey begins with you.

Conclusion

Integrating self-leadership and self-discovery creates an integrated approach to personal and professional development. By understanding and leading yourself, you can navigate your life with purpose, resilience, and confidence. This powerful combination enhances growth and positively impacts relationships, careers, and well-being. Through continuous self-discovery and effective self-leadership, you can unlock your full potential and achieve a fulfilling and successful life.

You are the hero in this story! Enjoy the journey!

Sources

I have included a detailed list of notes, references, and citations for each chapter in *The Power of Self-Leadership*. I trust that most readers will find this list to be sufficient. However, I also realize that literature changes over time, and the references for this book may need to be updated.

Furthermore, I fully expect that I have made a mistake somewhere—either in attributing an idea to the wrong person or not giving credit to someone where it is due. If you believe I have made an error, please email me at Doug@DouglasLSchmidt.com so I can fix the issue immediately. While the notes and citations in the book's printed version are fixed, I will update this page as new information becomes available.

Resources, Reference Material, and Technology

Chapter One—Self-Leadership and Discovery

Boyatzis, Richard PhD, and Annie Mckee PhD. 2008. *Becoming A Resonant Leader: Becoming a Resonant Leader: Develop Your Emotional Intelligence, Renew Your Relationships, Sustain Your Effectiveness*. Harvard Business Press. pp. 78-85.

Boyatzis, Richard PhD, and Annie McKee PhD. 2005. *Resonant Leadership*. Harvard Business Review Press. pp. 95-96.

Brown, Brene. 2018. *Dare to Lead*. Random House: pp 52, 58, 272.

Campbell, Joseph. 2010. *The Power of Myth*. Bantam Doubleday Dell Publishing Group.

Campbell, Joseph. 2008. *The Hero with a Thousand Faces (The Collected Works of Joseph Campbell.* New World Library.

Duarte, Nancy. 2010. *Resonate: Present Visual Stories that Transform Audiences.* John Wiley and Sons, pp. 32-47.

Greene, Robert. 2013. *Mastery.* Penguin Books

Sinek, Simon. 2011. *Start with Why: How Great Leaders Inspire Everyone to Take Action.* Portfolio, pp. 135-137.

Taylor, William. 2024. *Complete Biography of Jason Kelce: NFL Icon.* William Talyor.

Chapter Two—Discover Your Talents, Strengths, and Superpowers

Barron, Barbara, and Paul Tieger. 2021. *Do What You Are: Discover the Perfect Career for You Through the Secrets of Personality Type.* Little Brown, Spark. pp. 353-354.

Buckingham, Marcus. 2021. *Go Put Your Strengths to Work: 6 Powerful Steps to Achieve Outstanding Performance.* Free Press: pp. 20-24.

Rath, Tom. 2007. *Strengths Finder 2.0: A New and Upgraded Edition of the Online Test from Gallup's Now, Discover Your Strengths.* Gallup Press: pp. 8-23.

Chapter Three—Goal Setting Tips and Techniques

Hyatt, Michael. 2023. *Your Best Year Ever: A 5-Step Plan for Achieving Your Most Important Goals.* Gallup Press: pp. 17-23.

Markman, Art PhD. 2012. *Smart Thinking: Three Essential Keys to Solve Problems, Innovate, and Get Things Done by Art Markman.* Perigee Trade.

Chapter Four—Developing Your Learning Superpower

Oakley, Barbara, PhD, and Terrence Sejnowski PhD. 2018. *Learning How to Learn.* TarcherPerigee.

Oakley, Barbara, PhD. *"Learning How to Learn."* Coursera.Org. https://www.coursera.org/learn/learning-how-to-learn.

Oakley, Barbara, PhD. 2017. *Mindshift: Break Through Obstacles to Learning and Discover Your Hidden Potential.* TarcherPerigee.

Oakley, Barbara, PhD. *"Mindshift."* Coursera.Org. https://www.coursera.org/learn/mindshift.

Oakley, Barbara, PhD, Terrence Sejnoswki PhD, and Beth Rogowsky PhD. 2021. *Uncommon Sense Teaching.* TarcherPerigee.

Oakley, Barbara, PhD. *"Uncommon Sense Teaching."* Coursera.Org. https://www.coursera.org/specializations/uncommon-sense-teaching-certificate.

Pickard, Laurie. 2017. *Don't Pay for Your MBA: The Faster, Cheaper, Better Way to Get the Business Education You Need.* Amacom: pp. 33-47.

Chapter Five—Personal SWOT Analysis—Your Strategic Tool for Success

Mah, Mary. 2024. *The Ultimate Personal SWOT Analysis Guide.* Changemakers Publishing.

Rimm, Allison. 2013. *Joy of Strategy: A Business Plan for Life.* Bibliomotion.

Scott, Gini G. 2019. *10 Ways to Analyze Your Own Strengths, Weaknesses, Opportunities, and Threats.* Changemakers Publishing. Audio Book.

Chapter Six—Developing a Growth and Grit Mindset

Duckworth, Angela, PhD. 2016. *Grit: The Power of Passion and Perseverance.* Simon and Shuster: pp. 54-58.

Dweck, Carol, PhD. 2006. *Mindset: The New Psychology of Success.* Simon & Shuster: pp. 224-230.

Divine, Mark. 2014. *Unbeatable Mind: Forge Resiliency and Mental Toughness to Succeed at an Elite Level.* Random House: pp.188-196.

Chapter Seven—Developing Mental Strength

Carroll, Michael. 2008. *The Mindful Leader: Awakening Your Natural Management Skills Through Mindfulness Meditation.* Trumpeter: pp. 195-199.

Childre, Doc, Donna Beech, and Howard Martin. 2005. *Transforming Stress: The Heartmath Solution for Relieving Worry, Fatigue, and Tension.* New Harbinger Publications: pp. 22-30.

Mumford, George. 2016. *The Mindful Athlete.* Parallax Press: p. 59.

Rock, David PhD. 2020. *Your Brain At Work.* Harper Business: pp. 14-18.

Chapter Eight—Overcoming Procrastination Tools and Techniques

Cirillo, Francesco. 2018. *The Pomodoro Technique: The Acclaimed Time-Management System That Has Transformed How We Work.* Crown Currency: pp.30-49.

Oakley, B., PhD (2018). *Learning How To Learn.* TarcherPerigee.

Noteberg, Staffan. 2009. *Pomodoro Technique Illustrated: The Easy Way to Do More in Less Time.* Pragmatic Bookshelf: pp. 3-12.

Steel, Piers, PhD. 2010. *The Procrastination Equation: How to Stop Putting Things Off and Start Getting Stuff Done.* HarperCollins E-books: pp. 3-14.

Chapter Nine—Developing SMART Habits

Clear, James. 2018. *Atomic Habits: An Easy & Proven Way to Build Good Habits & Break Bad Ones.* Avery: pp. 196-204.

Duhigg, James. 2012. *The Power of Habit.* Random House. pp. 275-286.

Chapter Ten—SMART Networking

Wallace, Ed. 2010. *Business Relationships That Last.* Greenleaf Book Group: pp. 186-188.

Lowndes, Leil. 2009. *How to Instantly Connect with Anyone*. McGraw Hill: pp. 71-76.

Goleman, Dan. 2007. *Social Intelligence*. Bantam: pp. 82-101.

Ferrazzi, Keith. 2009, Who's Got Your Back?, Penquin Group: pp 26-29.

Chapter Eleven—Dealing With Toxic People

Sutton, Robert, PhD. 2018. *The Asshole Survival Guide: How to Deal with People Who Treat You Like Dirt*. Harper Business: pp. 161-162.

Goleman, Dan, PhD. 2005. *Emotional Intelligence: Why It Can Matter More Than IQ*. Bantam: pp. 59-65.

Sutton, Bob PhD. 2012. *Good Boss, Bad Boss: How to Be the Best . . . and Learn from the Worst*. Balance: pp. 238-239.

Chapter Twelve—Putting It All Together

Burchard, Brendon. 2018. *The High Performance Planner*. Hay House.

Burchard, Brendon. 2022. *High Performance Habits: How Extraordinary People Become That Way*. Hay House.

Chapter Two

The two most important days in your life are the day you are born and the day you find out why—Mark Twain—Twain, Mark. 2014. *Mark Twain on Common Sense: Timeless Advice and Words of Wisdom from America's Most-Revered Humorist.* Skyhorse

We cannot solve our problems with the same thinking we used when we created them.—Albert Einstein—Smith, David. 2021. *100 Inspirational Quotes By Albert Einstein That Will Change Your Life And Set You Up For Success.* Independently Published.

Chapter Three

"The greater danger for most of us lies not in setting our aim too high and falling short, but in setting our aim too low and achieving our mark."—Michelangelo—Italian Sculptor & Painter—Wallace, William. 2011. *Michelangelo: The Artist, the Man and His Times.* Cambridge University Press.

"A very great vision is needed, and the man who has it must follow it as the eagle seeks the deepest blue of the sky."—Chief Crazy Horse—Native American—Lakota Sioux Warrior—Marshall, Joseph. 2005. *The Journey of Crazy Horse: A Lakota History.* Penguin Books.

Chapter Four

Leadership and learning are indispensable to each other.—President John F. Kennedy—Dallek, Robert. 2004. *An Unfinished Life: John F. Kennedy, 1917—1963.* Back Bay Books.

The Journey of a thousand miles begins with a single step.—Lao Tzu—Chinese Philosopher & Writer—Ni, Hua Ching. 1995. *Complete Works of Lao Tzu: Tao Teh Ching & Hau Hu Ching.* Sevenstar Communications.

Intellectual growth should commence at birth and cease only at death.—Albert Einstein—Isaacson, Walter. 2008. *Einstein: His Life and Universe.* Simon and Schuster.

Thanks to my reading, I have never been caught flat-footed by any situation, never at a loss for how any problem has been addressed before. It doesn't give me all the answers, but it lights what is often a dark path ahead.—General James Mattis, USMC (Ret.) & former Secretary of Defense—Mattis, James, and Bing West. 2021. *Call Sign Chaos: Learning to Lead.* Random House Trade Paperbacks.

Chapter Five

Knowing yourself is the beginning of all wisdom.—Albert Einstein—Isaacson, Walter. 2008. *Einstein: His Life and Universe.* Simon and Schuster.

If you can't fly then run, if you can't run then walk, if you can't walk then crawl, but whatever you do you have to keep moving forward.—Martin Luther King—King, Martin Luther, and James Washington. 2003. *A Testament of Hope: The Essential Writings and Speeches.* Harper One.

If you know the enemy and know yourself, you need not fear the result of a hundred battles.—Sun Tzu—Tzu, Sun. 2007. *The Art Of War.* Filiquarian.

Action is the foundational key to all success.—Pablo Picasso—Spanish Artist and Sculptor—O'Brian, Patrick. 1994. *Picasso: A Biography.* W.W. Norton & Co.

Chapter Six

Attitude is a little thing that makes a big difference.—Winston Churchill—Prime Minister of England—Roberts, Andrew. 2018. *Churchill: Walking with Destiny.* Viking.

Chapter Seven

You have power over your mind—not outside events. Realize this, and you will find strength. — Marcus Aurelius—Stoic Philosopher—Aurelius, Marcus, and Gregory Hays. 2003. *Meditations.* Modern Library.

As much as we pump iron and we run to build our strength up, we need to build our mental strength up...so we can focus...so we can be in concert with one another.—Phil Jackson—World Championship Basketball

Coach—Jackson, Phil, and Hugh Delehanty. 2014. *Eleven Rings: The Soul of Success*. Penguin Books.

"Meditation is not evasion; it is a serene encounter with reality." Thích Nhất Hạnh—Hanh, Thich Nhat. *2016. How to Live: Boxed Set of the Mindfulness Essentials Series*. Parrallax Press.

I've seen firsthand the transformative power of mindfulness through the MBSR program. It's not just about managing stress; it's about reclaiming control over your life and finding peace in the present moment.— Michael Baime, M.D.—UPENN—Penn Program for Mindfulness.

Chapter Eight

If you want to stop procrastinating, you don't need more self-discipline, but a more effective way to manage your time.—Francesco Cirillo. Cirillo, Francesco. 2018. *The Pomodoro Technique*. Crown Currency.

Chapter Nine

Habit is either the best of servants or the worst of masters.—Seneca—Roman Stoic philosopher—Seneca. Seneca , Lucius Annaeus . 1969. *Letters from a Stoic*. Penquin Books.

There are only two days in the year that nothing can be done. One is called yesterday and the other is called tomorrow, so today is the right day to love, believe, do, and mostly live.—Dalai Lama—Tibetan Buddhist. Lama, Dalai. 2001. *Ethics for the New Millennium*. Riverhead Books.

Chapter Ten

The currency of real networking is not greed but generosity.—Keith Ferrazzi—Ferrazzi, Keith. 2014. *Never Eat Alone*. Crown Currency.

You can make more friends in two months by becoming genuinely interested in other people than you can in two years by trying to get other people interested in you.—Dale Carnegie—Carnegie, Dale. 1998. *How to Win Friends & Influence People*. Pocket Books.

Chapter 11—Dealing With Toxic People

Keep away from people who try to belittle your ambitions.—Mark Twain— Twain, Mark. 2014. *Mark Twain on Common Sense.* Skyhorse.

*When someone shows you who they are, believe them the first time.—Maya Angelou—*Smith, David. 2021. *100 Inspirational Quotes By Maya Angelou: A Boost Of Wisdom And Inspiration From The Legendary Poet.* Independent Publishing.

*When you don't confront the bad behavior of toxic people, you're inadvertently encouraging it. Stand up to toxicity, set clear boundaries, and surround yourself with positivity.—Bob Sutton—*Sutton, Bob. 2010. *Good Boss, Bad Boss: How to Be the Best... and Learn from the Worst.* Balance.

Chapter 12—Putting It All Together

*Any time you have an opportunity to make a difference in this world, and you don't, then you are wasting your time on Earth.—Roberto Clemente—Hall of Fame Baseball Player & Humanitarian—*Maraniss, David. 2007. *Clemente: The Passion and Grace of Baseball's Last Hero.* Simon and Schuster.

The first and best victory is to conquer yourself.—Plato—Greek Philosopher. Cooper, John. 1997 *Plato: Complete Works.* Hackett Publishing Company.

*You have power over your mind—not outside events. Realize this, and you will find strength.—Marcus Aurelius—Stoic Philosopher—*Hays, Gregory. 2020. *Meditations: A New Translation.* Independently Published.

Live as if you were to die tomorrow. Learn as if you were to live forever.— Mahatma Gandhi—*Ghandi, Mahatma. 2002. The Essential Gandhi: An Anthology of His Writings on His Life, Work, and Ideas.* Vintage

*Life is a journey, not a destination.—Ralph Waldo Emerson—*Smith, David. 2021. *100 Inspirational Quotes.* Independently published.

*The secret of getting ahead is getting started.—Mark Twain—American Writer, Humorist, & Essayist—*Twain, Mark. 1998. *The Wit and Wisdom of Mark Twain: A Book of Quotations.* Dover Publications.

Graphics and Technology

- Graphics—Canva—www.Canva.com
- Grammar Technology—Grammarly Premium—www.Gramarly.com
- Technology—ChatGPT—www.ChatGPT.com
- *Learning How to Learn*—Coursera.org
- *Mindshift*—Coursera.org

Acknowledgments

Writing a book takes a team, inspirational people, and role models. Special Thanks to the following for their support and inspiration.

Military Veterans—Col. John Church (USMC)—General Clifford Stanley (USMC)—General Joseph Harrington (US Army)—Captain Ralph Galati (US Airforce)—Sgt. Dennis Murphy (US Army)—Major Todd Parker (Army Ranger)—Joe Thomas, PhD (USNA)

In the book *A Soldier's Dream* by William Doyle, we reflect on the men and women who have served. I want to express my gratitude to the veterans who made the ultimate sacrifice, including Captain Travis Patriquin, Major Megan McClung, Specialist Vincent Pomante, and many others who have devoted themselves to serving this great nation.

Gary and Connie Patriquin—Gold Star Family and the many Gold Star Families whose family members who have paid the ultimate sacrifice.

Steve Harrison Publishing Team—Steve Harrison, Cristina Smith, Geoffrey Berwind, Valerie & Bob Costa, Geoffrey Berwind, Debby Englander, Shannon Hazel, Mary Lou Reid, Mary Lou Reid, Cathay Reta, Trish Ahjel Roberts, Darity Wesley

Editors—John Church, Cristina Smith, Valerie & Scott Costa

Graphic Designer—Christy Day

Early Reviewers—Paul Frank, Scott Messer, Jon Vogel, Walter Elliot, Glenn Hughes, Mark Iorio. Jim the Balloon Guy

Radnor and Tredyiffrin Libraries—Wayne PA

Panera Bread—Wayne, PA & Wilmington, DE

New Wayne Pizza—The Kontis Family

Career Consultant and Coach—Ruth Campbell

About the Author

 Douglas L. Schmidt is a dynamic leader and educator, passionately inspiring others to reach their full potential. With an MBA and a strong educational background, he blends academic insight with real-world experience to provide actionable leadership, learning, and personal growth strategies. His approach highlights the power of connections, fostering collaboration and mentorship to propel individual and team success. A steadfast believer in the growth mindset, Douglas champions resilience, adaptability, and continuous improvement as vital elements for overcoming challenges and achieving excellence.

His successful sales career spans Fortune 500 companies and entrepreneurial ventures, where he has mastered building trust and creating value in high-stakes environments. By combining strategic thinking with interpersonal skills, he consistently delivers outstanding results. Through his leadership, Douglas achieves measurable outcomes and inspires those around him to embrace a vision of innovation, connection, and the relentless pursuit of their goals.

THE POWER OF SELF-LEADERSHIP
FREE BONUSES & RESOURCES

COMPLIMENTARY STRATEGY SESSION

- Schedule a Time:
  - www.Calendly.com/DouglasLSchmidt
- No Charge

FREE SELF-LEADERSHIP WORKBOOK

A companion guide with exercises to apply your knowledge.

- Email me at: Doug@DouglasLSchmidt.com
- Subject Line - Self-Leadership Workbook

PROFESSIONAL SERVICES & RESOURCES

- Keynote and Public Speaking
- Professional and Personal Coaching
- Learning Design and Strategies
- Personal/Professional Networking Skills and Strategies

LET'S CONNECT - LINKEDIN CONNECTION

- https://www.linkedin.com/in/douglaslschmidt/

I would love to connect and hear about your comments, suggestions, and successes.

www.DouglasLSchmidt.com

www.ingramcontent.com/pod-product-compliance
Lightning Source LLC
Chambersburg PA
CBHW061727120626
46550CB00005B/1730